Peterson

First Guide

to

FISHES

of North America

Michael Filisky

Illustrated by
Sarah Landry

HOUGHTON MIFFLIN COMPANY
BOSTON   NEW YORK

Library of Congress Cataloging-in-Publication Data

Filisky, Michael.
Peterson first guide to fishes of North America.

Cover title: Peterson first guides. Fishes.
Includes index.
1. Fishes—North America—Identification.
I. Peterson, Roger Tory. II. Landry, Sarah.
III. Title.
QL625.F55 1989 597.097 88-32887
ISBN 0-395-91179-6

Printed in Italy

NIL 20 19 18 17 16 15

Editor's Note

In 1934, my *Field Guide to the Birds* first saw the light of day. This book was designed so that live birds could be readily identified at a distance, by their patterns, shapes, and field marks, without resorting to the technical points specialists use to name species in the hand or in the specimen tray. The book introduced the "Peterson System," as it is now called, a visual system based on patternistic drawings with arrows to pinpoint the key field marks. The system is now used throughout the Peterson Field Guide Series, which has grown to over thirty-five volumes on a wide range of subjects, from ferns to fishes, shells to stars, and animal tracks to edible plants.

Even though Peterson Field Guides are intended for the novice as well as the expert, there are still many beginners who would like something simpler to start with — a smaller guide that would give them confidence. It is for this audience — those who perhaps recognize a crow or a robin, a buttercup or a daisy, but little else — that the Peterson First Guides have been created. They offer a selection of the animals and plants you are most likely to see during your first forays afield. By narrowing the choices — and using the Peterson System — they make identification much easier. First Guides make it easy to get started in the field, and easy to graduate to the full-fledged Peterson Field Guides.

Roger Tory Peterson

Introducing the Fishes

How we see fishes depends on where we go and what we do. To the angler, the shopper, the aquarist, or the diver or underwater photographer, fishes are found at the end of a line, in the fish market, living behind glass, or free in their natural environment.

Fishes can be a source of sport, income, food, scientific knowledge, or enjoyment. Whether you spend months at sea as a crew member of a commercial fishing vessel or pass an occasional pleasant afternoon at the edge of a pond, fishes will affect your life.

About 2,200 species of fishes inhabit North American waters. Worldwide, there are more than 20,000 species of fishes, far more than of any other group of vertebrates (animals with backbones). This is not surprising when you realize that most of the Earth's surface is covered by fresh or salt water. Most of the other vertebrates, such as amphibians, reptiles, mammals, and birds, need solid ground for part or all of their lives.

Fishes usually are grouped into 3 major divisions: the jawless fishes, the cartilaginous fishes, and the bony fishes.

Although their ancestors were once the most abundant of vertebrates, the only living jawless fishes are the hagfishes and the lampreys (see pp. 10–11). The jaws of all other fishes evolved from the skeletal gill supports of the prehistoric ancestors of these fishes.

Cartilaginous fishes, including the sharks and the rays (see pp. 12–19), have skeletons made of flexible cartilage rather than bone. Most sharks are open-water predators; most rays live on the bottom. (Important exceptions include the Nurse Shark, which feeds on the bottom, and the Atlantic Manta, which swims in the open ocean.)

By far, the largest group is the bony fishes (see pp. 20–126), including over 97 percent of living fish species. As the name implies, these fishes have bony skeletons. Bony fishes can be found in nearly every possible aquatic habitat, from fresh to salt water, hot to cold water, and ocean to pond.

Fish Shapes

The shapes of fishes reveal much about their lives. Each shape gives the fish special advantages, but usually at the price of losing other abilities.

- Torpedo-shaped fishes with fins near the middle of the body are built for sustained speed. Although these fishes, including the mackerels and many of the sharks, can cruise at high speed for a long time, they are not very maneuverable.
- Torpedo-shaped fishes with fins far back on the body are usually lunge-predators. Barracudas and pikes, for example, wait motionless in the water, then capture their prey in a burst of speed.
- Flat fishes, such as flounders and skates, are well adapted for lying on the bottom. They often hide by covering the edges of their bodies with sand or gravel.
- Deep-bodied or compressed fishes are quite maneuverable but lack the ability to swim fast for long periods of time. These fishes, such as the freshwater sunfishes or the marine butterflyfishes, live among plants or corals where maneuverability is an important advantage.
- Boxy, bulky fishes, such as boxfishes or puffers, are quite maneuverable but cannot swim fast, even in short bursts. To protect themselves from predators, these fishes have developed armored bodies, as in the boxfishes, or special defensive behaviors such as the ability to inflate, as in the puffers.
- Eel-like fishes are specialized for moving through dense vegetation, hiding in rocky holes, or burrowing in soft bottoms. These fishes, such as the eels and gunnels, also have small scales and fins.

These are only a few of the many fish shapes. By watching fishes in an aquarium or in their underwater habitats, or by noticing where certain fishes are usually caught, you can probably make some good guesses about the relationship between a fish's shape and its way of life.

Parts of Cartilaginous Fishes

SHARKS
- The **nostrils** are for smelling.
- The **gill slits,** used for breathing, are on the sides.
- A pair of **pectoral fins** and a pair of **pelvic fins** steer the shark.
- The **dorsal and anal fins** provide stability during swimming.
- The male's **claspers** are used for internal fertilization of the female's eggs.
- The uneven **tail-fin lobes** are characteristic of sharks. They propel the shark through the water, keeping it from sinking to the bottom.

RAYS AND SKATES
- The **mouth** and **gill slits** are always on the underside of the body.
- The winglike **pectoral fins** are flapped during swimming.
- The back of a skate is often covered with spiny **thorns,** for protection.
- Skates have a thick, finned **tail**; rays have a thin, whiplike tail.

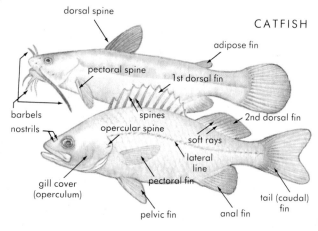

dorsal spine

CATFISH

adipose fin

pectoral spine

1st dorsal fin

barbels

spines

2nd dorsal fin

nostrils

opercular spine

soft rays

lateral line

gill cover (operculum)

pectoral fin

pelvic fin

anal fin

tail (caudal) fin

PERCHLIKE FISH

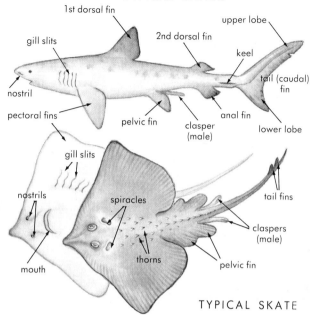

TYPICAL SHARK

1st dorsal fin
gill slits
2nd dorsal fin
upper lobe
keel
nostril
tail (caudal) fin
pectoral fins
pelvic fin
clasper (male)
anal fin
lower lobe

gill slits
nostrils
spiracles
tail fins
claspers (male)
thorns
mouth
pelvic fin

TYPICAL SKATE

Parts of Bony Fishes

- The **nostrils** are for smelling. Usually there are 4 nostrils, 2 on each side.
- The **gill cover** protects the gills. Often, it carries spines.
- **Barbels** around the mouth or chin of catfishes, cods, or Nurse Sharks are sensitive organs used for finding food.
- Some fishes have 1 **dorsal fin** on the back and some have 2. Often, the 1st dorsal fin is armed with spines, while the 2nd has soft fin rays.
- Fishes such as catfishes and trouts have a fleshy **adipose fin** behind their single dorsal fin.
- The **pectoral fins,** located just behind the gills, can have many functions. Depending on the species, they can be used for swimming, gliding, steering, or probing. Catfishes have sharp pectoral-fin spines.
- The **pelvic fins,** usually used for stability,

can be far back on the body or directly beneath the throat.

- The **anal fin** usually helps stabilize the fish's body while it swims. In the males of species that give live birth, the anal fin is often modified for fertilizing the eggs internally.
- The **tail fin,** or **caudal fin,** can be forked, rounded, or squared off. Usually, it is used for propelling the fish through the water. In some fishes, like the filefishes, the dorsal and anal fins function as propellers while the tail fin steers.
- The **lateral line,** which runs along the sides in most bony fishes, is part of a unique sensory system. With it, the fish can navigate by detecting the vibrations of animals or objects in the water.

We share many characteristics with fishes. Our eyes, skeletons, and many of our internal organs are very similar. We both have hearts, nerves, stomachs, and brains.

Many fish characteristics, however, are not shared by people. Some fishes have naked (unscaled) skin, but most are covered with protective scales. All fishes breathe water through their gills. Some, however, such as the lungfishes, which are not found in North America, have true lungs and are able to breathe air. Other fishes, such as the gars, gulp air into their gut or swim bladder.

The swim bladder is a unique organ found only in fishes. It is a sac in the body filled with air or other gases. In some fishes, such as the gars, it functions as a kind of lung. Most fishes, however, use their swim bladders as floats, to adjust their buoyancy. Sharks, which lack swim bladders, must keep swimming to stay afloat. Having a swim bladder frees the bony fishes from the need to swim constantly. Some fishes, such as midshipmen, make loud noises by vibrating their swim bladders. In many fishes the swim bladder also collects sounds, and thus allows the fish to hear well.

Many fish senses, such as hearing, touch, sight, and balance, are quite familiar to us. Some fish senses, however, are not shared by people.

The lateral-line system of fishes detects low-level vibrations in the water. Because of this, fishes can detect movement or reflections of their own vibrations, helping them to navigate. This is how blind fishes or fishes that live in total darkness keep from bumping into things. Schooling fishes, such as herrings, use their sophisticated lateral-line systems to maintain even spacing between school members.

Most fishes can detect electrical currents, such as those given off by muscles and nerves. This helps sharks and rays find food in murky water or when it is hidden in the sandy bottom. It may even help some fishes to navigate by following the Earth's magnetic field.

Though observing fishes can be an exciting pastime, there are some dangers to avoid. Very few fishes actually attack people in the water, but some can be quite dangerous. Some sharks, barracudas, and even bluefishes have inflicted serious wounds. Many fishes with strong jaws and sharp teeth can bite even after being caught.

Other parts of some fishes besides the jaws and teeth can inflict painful wounds. The gill covers of snooks and the spines of catfishes, scorpionfishes, and triggerfishes are sharp and, in some species, venomous. While the flesh of most fishes is delicious and healthful, some fishes contain dangerous toxins. Many puffers secrete powerful toxins in parts of their bodies. Other fishes pick up a toxin called ciguatera from their food and store it in their flesh, where it can poison people who eat it. Large, warm-water predators, such as barracudas or groupers, should probably not be eaten because of the danger of ciguatera poisoning.

We have described only a few of the more than 2,200 North American fish species. The most common, widespread, and easily found fishes from all habitats have been included, as well as some interesting examples of more unusual groups.

The sizes given are usually the maximum sizes that have been officially recorded. Unfortunately, these sizes are now rare or no longer seen for many fishes.

Jawless Fishes

These are the last surviving descendents of the jawless ancestors of all modern fishes. The jawless fishes are as often defined by what they lack (jaws, scales, pectoral and pelvic fins, a bony skeleton) as by what they have (skeletons of cartilage, a single nostril, an eel-like shape).

ATLANTIC HAGFISH To 2½ ft.

This eyeless, wormlike creature eats dead and dying fishes by entering through a natural opening in the victim's body, such as the mouth, and consuming the fish's internal organs. Because the Hagfish sometimes preys on fishes that are caught in a net or on a line, it is not popular with the fishing industry. As a defense, the Hagfish secretes large quantities of an obnoxious slime. To rid itself of the slime, it ties a knot in its body and slips it down to the tail. The Atlantic Hagfish is easily identified by its *eyeless head* and *star-shaped mouth* surrounded by 6 fleshy barbels. The Atlantic has only a single gill opening on each side. Found from Baffin Island, Canada, to North Carolina, the Atlantic Hagfish produces large, leathery eggs. A newly hatched Hagfish looks like a tiny version of the adult.

SEA LAMPREY To 3 ft.

Unlike the Atlantic Hagfish, the Sea Lamprey has *well-developed eyes* and 2 dorsal fins near its tail. It can also be identified by the 7 gill openings on each side and the *round, jawless mouth* lined with *horny teeth.* A young Lamprey hatches in fresh water, usually in a small stream, and lives in the mud for several years. As an adult it usually returns to its home in the sea. Since the late 19th century, however, a landlocked population of Sea Lamprey has lived in the Great Lakes, having entered through canals. The parasitic Sea Lamprey attaches itself to the side of a fish, rasps a hole with its tooth-covered tongue, and sucks out the blood and other body fluids.

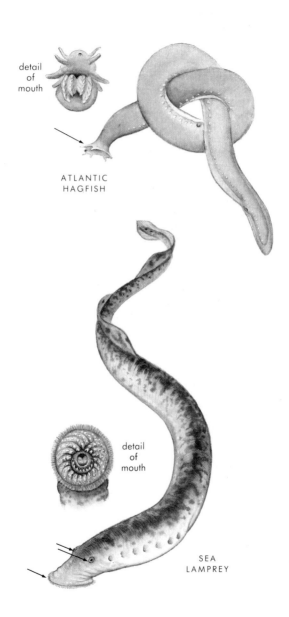

detail of mouth

ATLANTIC HAGFISH

detail of mouth

SEA LAMPREY

Sharks and Relatives

Sharks, along with rays, are called "carti-laginous fishes" because their skeletons are made of gristly cartilage rather than bone. Most sharks have 5–7 gill slits on each side, an upper tail lobe that is longer than the lower lobe, and a mouth on the underside of the snout. A shark's rough skin is covered with tiny, backward-pointing teeth. While some lay eggs, most sharks bear live young.

SCALLOPED HAMMERHEAD　　　To 14 ft.
Found near the surface from New Jersey to Brazil, this shark has a curved head with *distinct notches* that give the front a *scalloped shape.* The Scalloped Hammerhead gives birth to live young after nourishing them internally with an organ very much like the placenta and umbilical cord of mammals. Hammerheads can be dangerous.

TIGER SHARK　　　To 18 ft.
This large shark with a *short, rounded snout* is one of the most dangerous sharks to people. It is found near shore in the Atlantic from New England to Argentina and in the Pacific from southern California to Peru. It is omnivorous, taking nearly any prey.

SPINY DOGFISH　　　To 5 ft.
This small, harmless Atlantic shark is a common European food fish (the usual fish in English fish-and-chips) and finds its way to innumerable college laboratory dissection tables. The Spiny Dogfish is identified by the *strong spine in front of each dorsal fin* and by its white spots. It lives in the cool North Atlantic, from Labrador to North Carolina and off the coast of Europe.

PACIFIC ANGEL SHARK　　　To 5 ft.
This flattened, bottom-dwelling shark appears much like a ray. Unlike a ray, how-ever, the Angel Shark has pectoral fins that are *not connected to its head* and the gill slits are on its sides, not beneath its body. This fish is found over sand and mud, from Washington to Baja California.

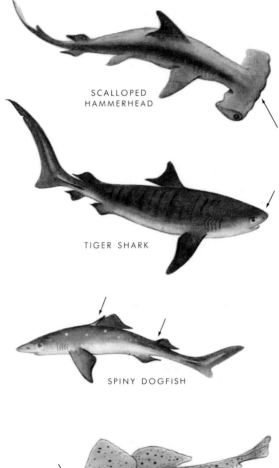

SCALLOPED
HAMMERHEAD

TIGER SHARK

SPINY DOGFISH

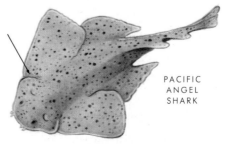

PACIFIC
ANGEL
SHARK

SHARKS, *continued*

WHALE SHARK   To 60 ft.

The Whale Shark is aptly named for its
huge size and its method of feeding.
Although it is the world's largest fish, it is
harmless to people. Its diet includes small
shrimps and fishes strained from the water.
Found in the open ocean (Atlantic: New
York to Brazil; Pacific: southern California
to South America), the Whale Shark is easily identified by its unique *checkerboard
pattern* of pale spots between thin lines.
This is also the only shark with a mouth at
the very front of its head.

BASKING SHARK   To 45 ft.

Second only to the Whale Shark in size, the
Basking Shark also filters tiny animals from
the water for food. It swims at the surface
with its huge mouth agape, straining water
through its comblike gill rakers. The water
then passes out through unusually long gill
slits. From a distance, a feeding Basking
Shark can be identified by the 3 body parts
breaking the surface: the rounded snout,
the large dorsal fin, and the *white-tipped
upper lobe* of the tail fin. The Basking
Shark's range is more northern than the
Whale Shark's (Atlantic: Newfoundland to
Florida; Pacific: Alaska to Baja California).

WHITE SHARK   To 21 ft.

Fear of the White Shark, inspired by horror
movies, is probably justified; hatred of it is
not. This shark is the largest hunting
shark, an important predator at the top of
the food chain. It should be avoided but re-
spected. The White Shark is found near both
coasts, in the Atlantic from Newfoundland
to Brazil, and in the Pacific from Alaska
to the Gulf of California. It has huge, triangular teeth and a *bluntly pointed snout.*

NURSE SHARK   To 14 ft.

Easily identified by its *2 barbels* and 2 dorsal fins of nearly equal size, the Nurse
Shark often lies on the bottom. It feeds on
crabs and small fishes. This harmless shark
is found in the Atlantic from Rhode Island
to Brazil, and in the Pacific from the Gulf of
California to Ecuador.

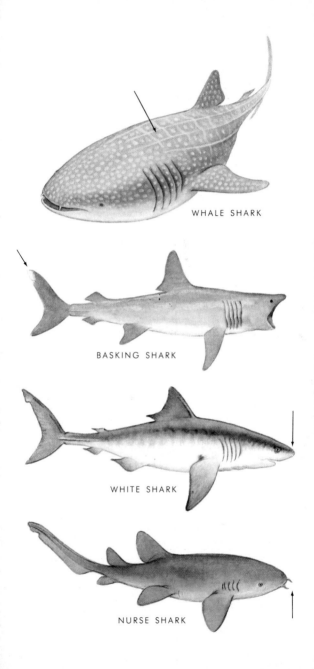

WHALE SHARK

BASKING SHARK

WHITE SHARK

NURSE SHARK

SEVENGILL SHARK To 9 ft.
  Throughout its range — British Columbia
  to Chile — this is the only shark with *7 gill
  slits* and a *single dorsal fin*. The Sevengill
  does not attack people but is dangerous
  when caught. It often has *small black
  spots*.

RAYS AND SKATES

  Well adapted for life on the bottom, rays and
  skates are flattened, with broad pectoral
  fins attached to the head. Like sharks, they
  have skeletons of cartilage, and skin covered with tiny teeth instead of scales.

SMALLTOOTH SAWFISH To 18 ft.
  Although it looks vaguely sharklike, a sawfish is, in fact, an elongated ray. As in all
  rays, the gill slits are beneath the body, not
  on the sides. The Smalltooth has 24 or
  more teeth along its *sawlike snout*, which
  is used to sift through sediment or to slash
  through schools of fish. This sawfish ranges
  from Chesapeake Bay to Brazil.

SHOVELNOSE GUITARFISH To 5½ ft.
  More sharklike than most rays, but more
  flattened than the Sawfish, the Shovelnose
  Guitarfish hunts for small invertebrates in
  shallow water, from San Francisco to the
  Gulf of California. It is identified by its *long,
  pointed snout*.

LESSER ELECTRIC RAY To 1½ ft.
  This little ray can jolt an unwary bather
  with about 37 volts of electricity from 2
  battery-like muscles on the sides of its
  head. This ray hunts worms in shallow
  water, from North Carolina to Argentina. It
  has a *rounded snout* and is covered with
  dark blotches and spots.

ATLANTIC STINGRAY To 2 ft.
  With a defensive weapon (a *grooved, venomous spine*) at the base of a *whiplike tail*,
  the Atlantic Stingray should be avoided.
  This ray is found in shallow water from
  Chesapeake Bay to the Gulf of Mexico. It is
  identified by its *pointed snout*.

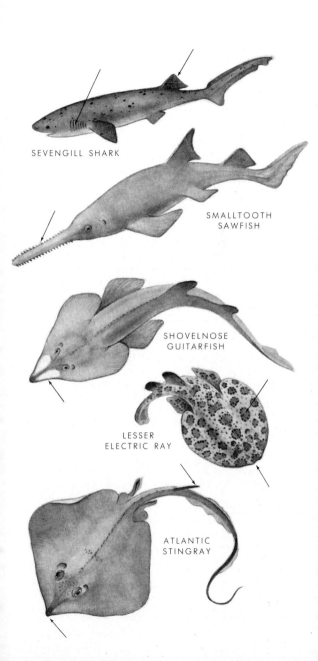

SEVENGILL SHARK

SMALLTOOTH
SAWFISH

SHOVELNOSE
GUITARFISH

LESSER
ELECTRIC RAY

ATLANTIC
STINGRAY

SKATES AND RAYS

LITTLE SKATE   To 1¾ ft.

Skates can be distinguished from their close relatives, the rays, by a fleshier tail bearing 1–2 small dorsal fins. Unlike the rays, which generally bear live young, skates lay eggs. Skate eggs are individually contained in leathery, pillow-shaped cases that are called "mermaid's purses" by beachcombers. This skate feeds on shrimps, clams, squids, and worms in shallow water. It lives in cool Atlantic waters from the Gulf of St. Lawrence to North Carolina. The Little Skate has no spines on the back and tail. Its upperside is covered with *many small, irregular spots.*

BIG SKATE   To 8 ft.

Aptly named, this is the largest Pacific skate. The Big Skate can also be identified by its triangular, pointed "wings" and its *2 prominent eyespots.* Like all skates, it prefers cool water; this skate ranges from the Bering Sea to Baja California. The wings of all skates, including the Big Skate, can be quite delicious. Unscrupulous fish dealers sometimes punch out round sections of skate wings and sell them as scallops.

ATLANTIC MANTA   To 22 ft. wide

This truly gigantic ray lives on some of the smallest forms of sea life, as do the largest sharks and whales. As the Manta swims, large quantities of water pass through its mouth and gills. *Peculiar flaps near the mouth* funnel in animals ranging from small fishes and shrimps to microscopic plankton, all of which are strained from the water. Like the eagle rays (not shown), the mantas have left behind the usual bottom-dwelling habits of the rays for a life of open-ocean swimming. The Atlantic Manta is a graceful swimmer and is normally harmless to people, but its great strength can make it dangerous when trapped or harpooned. This huge ray is found from New England to Brazil, usually near the surface of the open ocean. Despite its name, the Atlantic Manta is also found in the Pacific, from southern California to Peru.

18

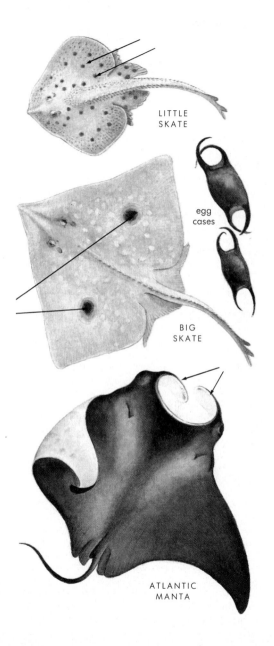

LITTLE
SKATE

egg
cases

BIG
SKATE

ATLANTIC
MANTA

Primitive Bony Fishes

The fishes on this page are survivors of some of the first groups of bony fishes to appear on earth. "Ancestral" might be a better term for these fishes, for their survival techniques are anything but primitive.

PADDLEFISH
To 7 ft.

With a *paddle-shaped snout* occupying ⅓ of its length, this fish could only have been called a paddlefish. Found in the deepest parts of the Mississippi River system, the Paddlefish swims with its huge mouth open wide, filtering small bits of food from the water. Its eggs make excellent caviar. There are 2 living paddlefish species: one in North America and one in China.

WHITE STURGEON
To 12½ ft.

"Primitive" features of sturgeons include *bony plates* in the skin and a tail with an *upper lobe that is larger* than the lower one. The White Sturgeon is found in rivers from Alaska to northern California and in the Pacific from Alaska to Baja California. It is prized for its meat as well as its caviar.

BOWFIN
To 2¾ ft.

About 100 million years ago, during the time of the dinosaurs, many kinds of bowfins thrived. Today's sole surviving species, the Bowfin, lives in the Great Lakes and Mississippi River system. It is distinguished by a large head, *tube-like nostrils*, a *single long dorsal fin*, and a slightly upcurved tail. The male is smaller than the female and has a *dark, orange-rimmed tail spot*.

LONGNOSE GAR
To 6 ft.

Gars are streamlined, with dorsal and anal fins set very far back. These effective ambush predators lie in wait, then lunge at passing fishes. The Longnose takes its name from its *very long snout*. Like other gars, it is covered with protective bony scales. This gar is found in quiet water from Quebec to Texas. In warm, stagnant water, it gulps air to supplement the oxygen taken from the water by its gills.

PADDLEFISH

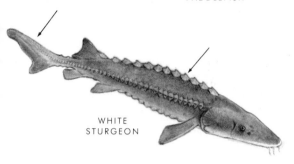

WHITE
STURGEON

BOWFIN

male

LONGNOSE GAR

Herrings and Relatives

This collection of families consists of small, silvery, schooling fishes. Most herrings have a sharp ridge of scales along the belly. Herrings swim open-mouthed in huge schools, filtering food from the water with their fine, comblike gill rakers. Herrings and their kin are crucial to the ocean food web: they eat tiny plankton and in turn are eaten by the larger fishes, birds, mammals, and people.

ATLANTIC HERRING To 14 in.

This very important commercial fish schools throughout the North Atlantic, from Greenland to North Carolina and on the European coast. The Atlantic Herring is somewhat slimmer than the similar Blueback Herring (not shown) and totally lacks the Blueback's spots. It is eaten fresh, pickled, or smoked.

GIZZARD SHAD To 16 in.

This fish is named for its muscular stomach. The freshwater Gizzard Shad is widespread throughout North America, east of the Rockies and south of the Great Lakes but is sometimes found in coastal salt water. The *dark shoulder spot* and the *long filament at the rear of the dorsal fin* make it easy to identify.

AMERICAN SHAD To 2½ ft.

This fish originally lived only in the Atlantic, from Labrador to Florida. In the 19th century it was introduced into the Pacific, where it now ranges from Alaska to Mexico. The American Shad stays near the coast, running up rivers to spawn. Its *dark shoulder spot* is usually followed by *several smaller spots*.

ALEWIFE To 15 in.

This fish has large eyes and a *single shoulder spot*. Like the American Shad, this coastal herring runs up rivers to spawn. Some alewives, such as those introduced into the Great Lakes, spend their entire lives in fresh water. Although alewives are seen as a nuisance in the Great Lakes, coastal populations are commercially important.

ATLANTIC HERRING

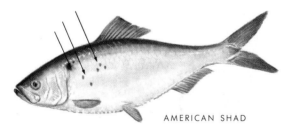

GIZZARD SHAD

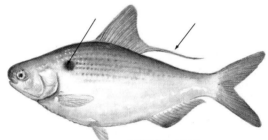

AMERICAN SHAD

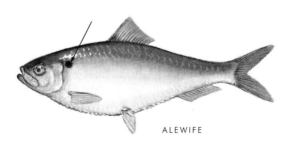

ALEWIFE

HERRINGS AND OTHERS

ATLANTIC MENHADEN To 1½ ft.
Like the American Shad, this fish has a dark shoulder spot followed by several smaller spots. It is distinguished by its *big, bony head* and *large mouth.* Found in enormous schools from Nova Scotia to Florida, the Menhaden supports a large fishing industry. It is used for fish meal and oil.

NORTHERN ANCHOVY To 9 in.
Unlike the herrings, which are closely related, anchovies have an *overhanging snout* and a *long lower jaw* that extends well behind the eyes. From British Columbia to Baja California, the Northern Anchovy is an important commercial fish as well as the main food source for many sea birds.

GOLDEYE To 1¾ ft.
The Goldeye and the Mooneye are the only members of the mooneye family. Similar to herrings, they have dorsal fins set farther back. True to its name, the Goldeye has large, *golden-yellow eyes.* It lives in quiet fresh water from the midwestern states to the Canadian Northwest Territories.

TARPON To 8 ft.
Although the Tarpon looks like a gigantic herring, it is more closely related to the eels! (Both the Tarpon and the eels have larval young that look like long, translucent leaves.) The Tarpon is silvery, with *extremely large scales* and a *long filament at the rear of its dorsal fin.* Due to its sensational fighting and leaping ability, the Tarpon is one of the most highly prized sport fishes from North Carolina to Brazil.

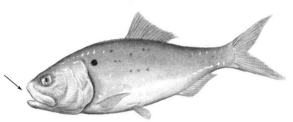

ATLANTIC MENHADEN

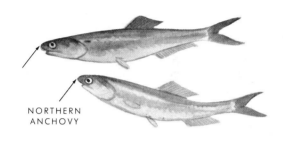

NORTHERN
ANCHOVY

GOLDEYE

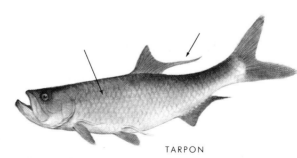

TARPON

Eels

Freshwater eels, conger eels, snake eels, and morays are all separate families within the larger grouping (order) of eels. All have the typical long, serpentine eel form.

AMERICAN EEL To 4½ ft.

The American Eel makes a reverse breeding journey compared to the salmon: it lives in fresh water and spawns in the sea. This eel has a *protruding lower jaw* and scales embedded in the skin.

CONGER EEL To 7½ ft.

The Conger differs from the American Eel in having a *shorter lower jaw* and a dorsal fin that begins farther forward. Its long dorsal fin is continuous with the anal fin and is pale with a dark edge. The Conger inhabits shallow water from Cape Cod to Florida.

PACIFIC SNAKE EEL To 3½ ft.

Like all snake eels, this species has a *spiky, finless tail* used for burrowing backwards into the bottom. The Pacific Snake Eel lives in shallow water, from California to Peru. It can be identified by its random dark spots.

GREEN MORAY To 8 ft.

The largest moray, found on reefs, rocks, and pilings from New Jersey to Brazil. This moray has no other markings on its *uniformly green body.* Like other morays, the Green has an uncovered gill opening and no pectoral fins. The Green Moray is territorial, but usually it will attack only if its home hole is invaded. It is a popular exhibit fish in large public aquaria.

CALIFORNIA MORAY To 5 ft.

Like most morays, the California Moray leaves its hole to hunt at night. The only moray in its range, it is found on reefs, from northern California to Baja California. Its lack of pectoral fins and uncovered gill opening identify it as a moray. Divers should never carelessly poke into crevices and holes that could be moray homes. This eel will bite with sharp teeth if provoked.

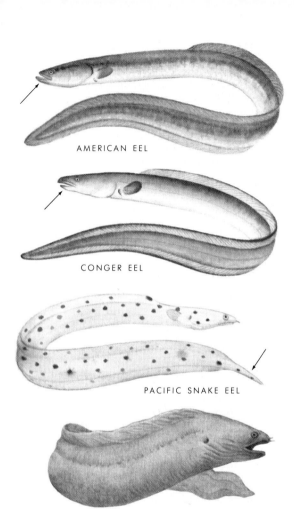

AMERICAN EEL

CONGER EEL

PACIFIC SNAKE EEL

GREEN MORAY

CALIFORNIA MORAY

Salmon, Trouts, and Others

This family includes some of the most popular sport and food fishes. Native to cool waters in the northern hemisphere, they have been widely introduced south of the equator. Salmon migrate from the sea to spawn in fresh water; most trouts and whitefishes spend their entire lives in fresh water. All are streamlined and have a small, fleshy adipose fin behind the dorsal fin.

CHINOOK SALMON   To 4 ft.

The largest salmon, the Chinook (or King) is found in the Pacific from the Bering Sea to San Diego. It spawns in streams north of the Sacramento. The upper body and *both lobes* of the tail fin *are spotted* and *the gums are black.* The Chinook is caught both at sea and in its river runs.

SOCKEYE SALMON   To 2½ ft.

The Sockeye or Red Salmon is found in the Pacific from the Bering Sea to Los Angeles; it spawns from the Columbia River north. This salmon *lacks spots on the tail fin.* Breeding adults are bright red with pale green heads. This is the most valuable commercial salmon.

COHO SALMON   To 3 ft.

The Coho or Silver Salmon has *spots only on the back* and the *upper lobe* of the tail fin. *The gums are white.* Found at sea from the Bering Strait to Baja California, the Coho spawns in streams north of Monterey, California. It has also been introduced into the Great Lakes.

ATLANTIC SALMON   To 4½ ft.

Unlike the many Pacific species, the Atlantic Salmon usually survives after spawning to return to the sea. It can be identified by a lack of spots on the tail fin and *numerous X-shaped spots* on the body. Breeding males develop upward-hooking lower jaws. Pollution of its spawning habitat is a great threat to the Atlantic Salmon. Efforts to reintroduce it to New England rivers, however, are meeting with some success.

breeding male

CHINOOK SALMON

breeding male

SOCKEYE SALMON

breeding male

COHO SALMON

breeding male

ATLANTIC SALMON

TROUTS AND OTHERS

BROOK TROUT To 1½ ft.

This colorful trout sports a marbled back, multicolored side spots, a white or reddish belly, and *ruddy pectoral, pelvic, and anal fins* with *white leading edges.* The natural range of the Brook Trout stretches from the Great Lakes to the Atlantic and from Labrador to Georgia. It has also been introduced to streams in the high Rockies, where it is a favorite game fish.

BROWN TROUT To 4 ft.

Introduced from Europe a century ago, the Brown Trout tolerates warmer water than our native North American species do. It also differs in having a squared-off (unforked) tail. The Brown Trout is indeed brown, with pale-ringed spots. It lives in fresh water throughout warm-temperate North America. Small populations also inhabit the Atlantic.

RAINBOW TROUT To 3½ ft.

A reddish side stripe and a profusion of small black spots (especially on the tail fin) identify the Rainbow Trout. Native to western lakes and streams from Alaska to Baja California, this favorite sport fish has been introduced across North America. Steelheads (sea-run Rainbow Trout) lack the stripe but still have the spots.

LAKE TROUT To 4 ft.

The Sea Lamprey (see p. 12) destroyed the Great Lakes population of the Lake Trout. It still flourishes, however, in deep, cold lakes throughout Canada, Alaska, and New England. *Pale spots* cover the Lake Trout's body. Its tail is deeply forked.

LAKE WHITEFISH To 2 ft.

Silvery and flat-sided, this fish looks like a herring, but the small adipose fin reveals its kinship to trouts. It is a delicious and important food fish throughout Canada, Alaska, and the Great Lakes. The Lake Whitefish has a *small mouth, thick lips, overhanging snout,* and *slightly humpbacked appearance.*

BROOK TROUT

BROWN TROUT

RAINBOW TROUT

LAKE TROUT

LAKE WHITEFISH

RAINBOW SMELT To 1 ft.

This small relative of the trouts (note the *troutlike adipose fin*) lives in streams and in coastal salt water, from the Great Lakes through New England to the Canadian Maritimes. Often caught by ice fishing, it is also an important food fish.

PIKES

Four of the 5 pikes found in the world live in North America. With fins set far back and big toothy jaws, these large fishes are well equipped to lunge at their prey — smaller fishes, aquatic mammals, and waterfowl. Most pikes hunt by sight, and so prefer clear water.

NORTHERN PIKE To 4½ ft.

Found in weedy lakes and streams from the Arctic Ocean to Missouri, the Northern Pike also dwells in northern Europe and Asia (the most extensive natural range of any freshwater fish). Its pattern of *pale spots* conceals it among water weeds, from which it lunges at its prey. Only the Muskellunge is more popular with anglers.

MUSKELLUNGE To 6 ft.

The highly prized "Muskie" lives in lakes in the general Great Lakes area. It has a broad head and *dark blotches* (sometimes diagonal bars) on the body. Like all pikes, the Muskellunge feeds on fishes and waterfowl.

CHAIN PICKEREL To 2½ ft.

Covered with *pale spots*, a Chain Pickerel can be distinguished from a young Northern Pike by the *deeply forked tail* and the dark bar under each eye. This pickerel lives in clear lakes and ponds along the eastern seaboard and in the South. It is especially popular for ice fishing.

GRASS PICKEREL To 1 ft.

This fish, the smallest of the pikes, lives throughout the Mississippi River system. It can be identified by the *thin vertical lines* on its sides. The Grass Pickerel often interbreeds with the Chain Pickerel.

RAINBOW SMELT

NORTHERN PIKE

MUSKELLUNGE

CHAIN PICKEREL

GRASS PICKEREL

Carps, Minnows, and Suckers

Carps and minnows comprise one of the largest fish families (with some of the smallest members). Suckers make up a small family closely related to carps and minnows. Primarily freshwater fishes, the members of both families have a single dorsal fin. Lacking jaw teeth, they have grinding teeth in the throat.

GOLDFISH To 2½ ft.

The Goldfish has a single dorsal spine. All Goldfish in North American ponds or streams are feral (domestic animals gone wild). The Goldfish ancestor was a drab, wild Chinese carp. After centuries of captive breeding, the gold, orange, white, black, and mottled forms popular today were developed. If Goldfish are allowed to go wild for several generations, their offspring often become dull olive again. The Goldfish is hardy enough to outcompete many native fishes; it should not be released into the wild.

COMMON CARP To 2½ ft.

Originally from the Old World, this fish is another North American newcomer. It is easily caught but not highly valued for food. This carp is easily recognized by the *2 pairs of barbels* on the mouth. Found from southern Canada to Mexico, the Common Carp can withstand very stagnant water.

QUILLBACK To 2 ft.

With its *stiff, high dorsal fin*, the Quillback is well named. Like all suckers, it has thick lips and a small head. The Quillback inhabits muddy water in the Mississippi River system and southwestern Canada.

SMALLMOUTH BUFFALO To 3 ft.

This large sucker has an *arched back*, sometimes with a forward ridge. Found in rivers and lakes throughout the Mississippi River system and Texas, the Buffalo is not popular for sport but has some commercial value.

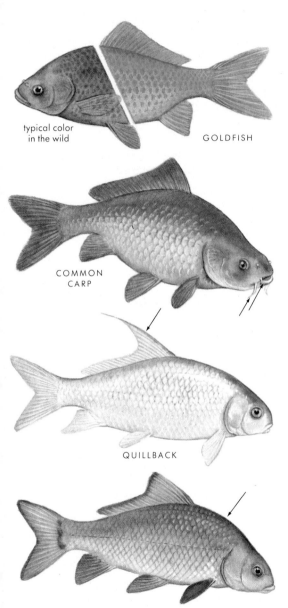

typical color
in the wild

GOLDFISH

COMMON
CARP

QUILLBACK

SMALLMOUTH BUFFALO

MINNOWS, *continued*

ROUNDTAIL CHUB   To 1½ ft.

Limited to, but common in, the Colorado
River system, the Roundtail Chub prefers
warm, slightly muddy water. This slender
little minnow has a relatively *large mouth*
with *no barbels.* The male Roundtail has
reddish sides.

HITCH   To 1 ft.

The Hitch is found only in California, in
Clear Lake and several rivers. It usually prefers warm water with plant life where it can
hide. Its ability to avoid predators has
enabled the Hitch to survive the introduc-
tion of many non-native fishes into its
range. It has a *very small mouth* and a
characteristic *long, thin section* before the
tail fin.

GOLDEN SHINER   To 1 ft.

Named for the somewhat *golden tint* of its
back, the Golden Shiner is very common in
clear fresh water east of the Rockies. It has
a rather arched back and a ridge between
the pelvic and anal fins. The Golden Shiner
is often encountered in bait shops as well as
in streams. Either way, it is eagerly sought
by many game fishes.

EMERALD SHINER   To 4 in.

This *very slender and compressed* little
minnow swims in schools in the open water
of large lakes and streams throughout the
Mississippi River system, the Great Lakes
region, and south-central Canada. The
Emerald Shiner is a favorite food of many
game fishes, and so it is often used as bait.

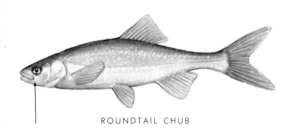

ROUNDTAIL CHUB

HITCH

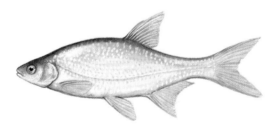

GOLDEN SHINER

EMERALD SHINER

COMMON SHINER   To 6 in.

True to its name, the Common Shiner is quite common, but only in the cool waters within its range (New England to the upper Midwest). This shiner will tolerate only cool, clear, clean water. The decline of this fish can be the first indicator of silting or pollution of a stream.

SPECKLED DACE   To 4 in.

This is a common minnow in creeks, rivers, springs, and lakes west of the Continental Divide, from Canada to Arizona. It has a *speckled body* with a characteristic *dark side stripe.* Isolated in many small streams and springs, the Speckled Dace has developed a number of races or subspecies with slightly different shapes or markings.

SPOTTAIL SHINER   To 6 in.

This little shiner takes its name from the *small spot at the base* of the tail fin. It lives in large lakes and rivers, from the East Coast through the Great Lakes region to the Canadian Northwest Territories. This is a very popular bait minnow, especially in the Great Lakes region.

BLUNTNOSE MINNOW   To 4 in.

The slender little minnow does indeed have a *blunt nose.* The Bluntnose has a *dark crosshatch pattern,* a side stripe, and a dark spot at the base of the tail fin. This wide-ranging minnow lives in small rivers and lakes, from the Great Lakes region to the Gulf of Mexico.

COMMON SHINER

SPECKLED DACE

SPOTTAIL SHINER

BLUNTNOSE MINNOW

MINNOWS AND OTHERS

FATHEAD MINNOW   To 4 in.

The Fathead has a very large, round head with a blunt snout. The *first ray* of its dorsal fin is *short* and there is a characteristic *dark spot* on the tail fin. Wide ranging for a minnow, the Fathead inhabits clear ponds, lakes, and streams throughout central Canada and the U.S. east of the Rockies, except for the Southeast.

SOUTHERN REDBELLY DACE   To 3 in.

This handsome little minnow is found in the northern part of the Mississippi River system. Not common in large bodies of water, it prefers clear and cool streams and springs. The Southern Redbelly's sides are decorated with *black and cream stripes*. A dark tail-fin spot is formed by an extension of one of the stripes. During the spring breeding season, the male's belly glows bright red, giving the species its name.

HORNYHEAD CHUB   To 10 in.

The breeding male Hornyhead has a *bright red spot* behind each eye and many *fleshy growths* on the head. Found from the Great Lakes region and the upper Mississippi River area west to Wyoming, it prefers clear creeks and small streams with gravel bottoms. Populations of the Hornyhead Chub have declined in recent years, as development and agricultural run-off have silted its once-clear habitat.

CENTRAL MUDMINNOW   To 5 in.

Not true minnows, mudminnows are, in fact, closely related to the pikes (p. 34). Like the true minnows, the Central Mudminnow is small, and is often used for bait. It can be distinguished by its *rounded tail*. The mottling of the sides is often arranged into bars. Ranging through the Great Lakes region and the upper Mississippi area, the Central Mudminnow prefers the cool, weedy water of bogs, swamps, and slow streams.

FATHEAD MINNOW

breeding male

SOUTHERN REDBELLY DACE

male

HORNYHEAD CHUB

CENTRAL MUDMINNOW

SUCKERS

WHITE SUCKER   To 2 ft.
The White Sucker is found throughout the
central U.S. and most of Canada — the widest range of any sucker. Like all suckers, it
has thick lips covered with many fleshy
growths. With these sensitive "feelers," it
probes in the gravel for worms and other
small prey, sucking them up with its powerful mouth. The White Sucker is not really
white, but yellowish with a brassy sheen.

SACRAMENTO SUCKER   To 1½ ft.
This sucker has a characteristic *faint reddish stripe*. The Sacramento Sucker lives
only in the Sacramento–San Joaquin River
drainage. Unlike many river fishes, this fish
simply scatters its eggs rather than scooping out a gravel nest. The young avoid being
swept away by the current by burrowing
into the river bottom between large pebbles.

NORTHERN HOG SUCKER   To 2 ft.
For a sucker, this is quite a handsome fish.
Its *dark brown mottlings* are often arranged
into indistinct saddles. Found from the
Great Lakes region to Louisiana and the
Middle Atlantic states, the Northern Hog
Sucker prefers clear, swift streams. Most
suckers, including the Northern Hog, can-
not tolerate unclear water. For this reason,
they are threatened by pollution.

GOLDEN REDHORSE   To 2 ft.
This fish can be identified by its *golden-
bronze color*. The range of this sucker covers the entire Midwest, extending into parts
of the South and the Middle Atlantic states.
The Golden Redhorse prefers slow creeks
and streams, and is more tolerant of muddy
water than most suckers are. Suckers are
not prized as sport fish, but they can be a
real challenge for even an experienced
angler. With their sensitive lips, they can
often detect the hook in the bait and avoid
it.

WHITE SUCKER

SACRAMENTO SUCKER

NORTHERN HOG SUCKER

GOLDEN REDHORSE

Catfishes

With their sensitive barbels, small eyes, and excellent sense of hearing, catfishes are especially well adapted to life after dark or in muddy water. A typical North American catfish has a flattened head, a scaleless body, a small dorsal fin, and a small adipose fin between the dorsal fin and the tail. Many catfishes are prized for food and sport, but anglers should beware of their sharp fin spines.

YELLOW BULLHEAD   To 1½ ft.

This catfish is common in ponds, lakes, and the sluggish backwaters of streams, in southeastern Ontario and throughout the eastern states except for New England. Like all bullheads, the Yellow has 4 pairs of barbels. The chin barbels are *yellow to white*. Best caught at night, the Yellow Bullhead is a good sport and food fish.

BLACK BULLHEAD   To 1½ ft.

Found throughout the central states and southern Canada, the Black Bullhead prefers slow-moving, muddy water. Because it is more tolerant of silty or polluted water than other catfishes are, it is quite common. Similar in form to the Yellow Bullhead, the Black Bullhead is distinguished by its *grayish black* or spotted chin barbels.

CHANNEL CATFISH   To 3½ ft.

This is the king of North American food and sport catfishes. Its large size and firm flesh have made the Channel Catfish popular with anglers, commercial fishermen, and diners. In the South, this catfish is profitably raised in large artificial ponds on fish farms. Young Channel Catfish are covered with *dark spots*, which disappear with age. This catfish has 4 pairs of barbels and a *deeply forked tail*. The natural range of this fish covers the central and southern states and southern Canada, but it has been widely introduced elsewhere.

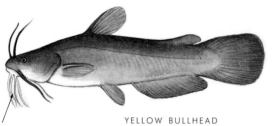

YELLOW BULLHEAD

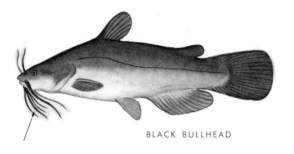

BLACK BULLHEAD

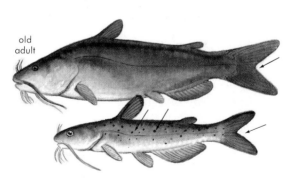

old
adult

CHANNEL CATFISH

CATFISHES, *continued*

TADPOLE MADTOM   To 4½ in.
The venomous pectoral-fin spines of this little catfish can inflict a very painful wound. The size and shape of a tadpole, this fish has an unusual, *keel-shaped adipose fin*, continuous with the tail fin. The Tadpole Madtom is found throughout the eastern states except in the Appalachians. This shy little catfish nests in dense vegetation and sometimes hides in empty cans.

FLATHEAD CATFISH   To 4½ ft.
With its darkly mottled body, squarish tail fin with a *white upper lobe*, and flattened head, the Flathead looks like no other North American catfish. Found in large rivers and streams from the Mississippi River area to the Rockies, this large catfish is popular for food. The young sometimes hide under flattened stones in shallow water.

WALKING CATFISH   To 14 in.
The Walking Catfish is a classic example of the dangers of introducing exotic (non-native) species into unfamiliar territory. Imported from Asia for the home aquarium trade, it escaped from south Florida fish farms into local waterways. Its ability to breathe air and "walk" between ponds and the absence of its natural predators give the Walking Catfish an advantage over native Floridian fishes. In many areas it has seriously damaged populations of native fishes. It is unmistakable, with its *long dorsal and anal fins*, small rounded tail fin, long barbels, and tiny eyes. It is frequently found in a pink albino form.

GAFFTOPSAIL CATFISH   To 3 ft.
One of the few marine catfishes, the Gafftopsail is found in shallow coastal waters from North Carolina to Brazil. It is identified by its characteristic *high dorsal fin*, long pectoral fins, and deeply forked tail. The Gafftopsail has only 2 pairs of barbels. Anglers should avoid the long, sharp dorsal- and pectoral-fin spines. The male protects the eggs and young in his mouth for as long as 3 months.

TADPOLE MADTOM

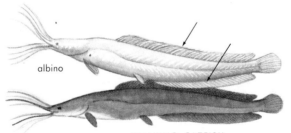

FLATHEAD CATFISH

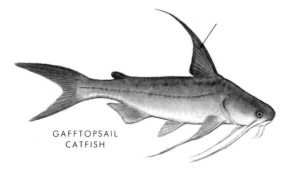

albino

WALKING CATFISH

GAFFTOPSAIL
CATFISH

Perchlike Fishes

SOUTHERN CAVEFISH   To 3 in.

A member of the peculiar North American cavefish family, the Southern Cavefish inhabits a lightless world in dark caves and underground pools in several southern states. This fish *lacks eyes* and skin color; its pinkish hue is a result of the blood showing through the skin. It also lacks pelvic fins. The Southern Cavefish navigates by using its sensitive skin growths, which also help it find food. Adult cavefishes carry their eggs in their gill chambers and protect the young by keeping them there when they first hatch.

PIRATE PERCH   To 4½ in.

The Pirate Perch is the only surviving member of a family that was common in prehistoric times. Found in still, weedy waters in the Mississippi River area and along the Atlantic coastal plain, it emerges from the cover of vegetation to feed at night. The Pirate Perch has a single dorsal fin, a small spine on the gill cover, and a rounded tail with 1 or 2 *dark bars* at the base.

TROUT-PERCH   To 6 in.

This little fish is neither a trout nor a perch. It does, however, have a perchlike form and a *troutlike adipose fin*. Two lines of *dark blotches* are found on the upper half of its body. Found in lakes and streams from Alaska to the upper Mississippi River system, the Trout-perch is an important prey species for Lake Trout and other game fishes.

SOUTHERN CAVEFISH

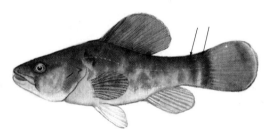

PIRATE PERCH

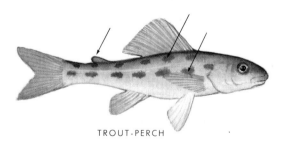

TROUT-PERCH

Toadfishes and Midshipmen

Members of this family of squat, unusual bottom-dwellers inhabit the shallow water of both coasts. With their muddy coloration and eyes on the top of the head, these fishes are well adapted to life on the bottom. Anglers should beware of their powerful jaws. Many toadfishes and midshipmen communicate with loud sounds, made by vibrating the swim bladder. The males vigorously guard the eggs, which are laid within small rock caves or objects such as pipes or cans.

OYSTER TOADFISH   To 15 in.

This is a tough fish. It can survive several hours out of water, can tolerate polluted water, and can deliver a nasty bite to the careless angler. The Oyster Toadfish waits among weeds or litter, camouflaged by its blotchy pattern. Unwary small fishes, crabs, and worms are snapped up by its large mouth. This fish has *fleshy flaps* on both lips and *bars* on the fins. It is found in shallow water, from Cape Cod to Florida.

PLAINFIN MIDSHIPMAN   To 15 in.

The midshipmen are among the very few bioluminescent fishes that live in salt water. Bioluminescence, the ability to glow in the dark, is usually found in denizens of the deep sea. In midshipmen, the light comes from rows of small organs called *photophores*, which resemble the rows of buttons on a naval midshipman's uniform. True to the other part of its name, the Plainfin has plain, *unspeckled fins*. It is found from Alaska to the Gulf of California.

Clingfishes

NORTHERN CLINGFISH   To 6 in.

Ranging from Alaska to southern California, the Northern Clingfish preys on small mollusks and crustaceans in the rocky intertidal zone. Like all clingfishes, it holds onto rocks with a *suction disk* formed of modified pelvic fins. This disk keeps the fish securely anchored in the strong tidal currents. The Northern Clingfish has *dark marbling* over a brown to cherry-red body.

OYSTER TOADFISH

PLAINFIN MIDSHIPMAN

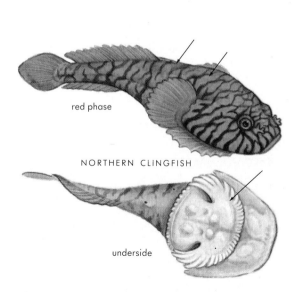

red phase

NORTHERN CLINGFISH

underside

Anglerfishes

Millions of years before people first took up rods and reels, the anglerfishes were using artificial lures to attract their prey. Their fishing gear consists of a "pole" and fleshy lure made from the modified first ray of the dorsal fin. Many anglerfishes are small fishes that live in the deep sea, but some, like the huge Goosefish, can be found in shallow water.

GOOSEFISH   To 4 ft.

The Goosefish seems, at first sight, to be all mouth. Its large head and toothy mouth allow it to swallow prey nearly as large as itself. Occasionally, diving birds such as cormorants have been found in the stomachs of Goosefish. The *fleshy tabs* along the head and body of this fish help it blend in with the bottom while the rod and dangling lure attract its prey. The Goosefish is a flattened bottom-dweller, found in shallow to moderately deep water from the Bay of Fundy to northern Florida. Its delicious, firm, white tail meat is sold as "monkfish."

SARGASSUMFISH   To 6 in.

The Sargassumfish is always found among floating sargassum weed, from New England to Brazil. This little anglerfish has a mottled pattern and fleshy tabs on its belly and chin that perfectly mimic the pattern and form of sargassum weed, rendering the fish nearly invisible to predator and prey alike. The Sargassumfish is a popular aquarium fish.

PANCAKE BATFISH   To 4 in.

Batfishes are related to the anglerfishes. With their flattened, disk-shaped body, batfishes are very well adapted to life on the bottom. This batfish hides in the sand during the day, and swims at night by "rowing" with its oarlike pectoral fins. It is quite circular, with a *short snout*. Its pectoral and tail fins are covered with *dark bars*. The Pancake Batfish lives over sand, from North Carolina to Florida and throughout the Gulf of Mexico.

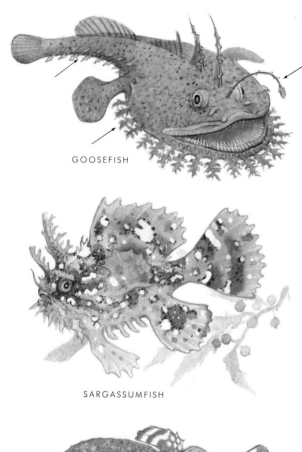

GOOSEFISH

SARGASSUMFISH

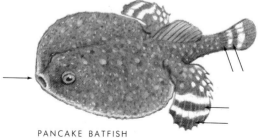

PANCAKE BATFISH

Cods and Relatives

Cods school throughout the world's cold oceans. These important commercial food fishes provide food and income for millions of people.

ATLANTIC COD
To 6 ft.

Found near the bottom in cold water from Greenland to Cape Hatteras, the Atlantic Cod also lives off the coast of Europe. It has a *well-developed chin barbel*, 3 dorsal fins, and 2 anal fins, and is covered with *spots*. Millions of pounds of this cod are harvested annually, but it is also a popular sport fish. The firm, white flesh of this fish is eaten fresh, frozen, salted, or dried.

HADDOCK
To 3½ ft.

The Haddock is even more highly valued as a food fish than the Atlantic Cod. Unfortunately, stocks of the Haddock have been depleted by overfishing. It lives in deeper water than the Cod, from Nova Scotia to Cape Hatteras. The first of its 3 dorsal fins is *high and pointed* and its shoulder area bears a *dark blotch*.

WHITE HAKE
To 4 ft.

All hakes have a tall 1st dorsal fin followed by a long 2nd dorsal fin. The pelvic fins have long, sensitive filaments. The White Hake has a *pale lateral line*. It lives over muddy bottoms, from Nova Scotia to Cape Hatteras. A good food fish, the White Hake is not marketed as widely as are some other members of the cod family.

PACIFIC TOMCOD
To 1 ft.

This small cod ranges from the Bering Sea to central California. Though it is not abundant enough to support an important commercial fishery, it is quite popular with anglers. The Pacific Tomcod is a slender fish with a *small chin barbel* and a *pointed 1st dorsal fin*. The edges of its fins are dusky.

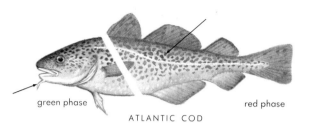

green phase   red phase

ATLANTIC COD

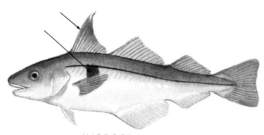

HADDOCK

WHITE HAKE

PACIFIC TOMCOD

CODS AND OTHERS

POLLACK
To 3½ ft.

Because its light flesh is laced with small, dark veins, the Pollack is not as popular as the Atlantic Cod. However, it is an important food fish. Fortunately for the fishing industry, the Pollack is often abundant when the Atlantic Cod is scarce. It is somewhat silvery, with no marks or spots, and has a *projecting lower jaw*, usually *without a chin barbel*. The Pollack ranges over rocky bottoms, from the Gulf of St. Lawrence to New Jersey.

BURBOT
To 3 ft.

This is the only freshwater member of the cod family. Ranging from the Arctic to the upper Mississippi River region, the Burbot prefers deep, cold rivers and lakes. It is very elongate and has a *long, slender chin barbel*. Both the 2nd dorsal fin and the anal fin are quite long. Only the pelvic fins are pale, the other fins being darkly mottled. The Burbot has the amazing habit of spawning in the winter, under the ice.

OCEAN POUT
To 3½ ft.

This long, eel-like fish belongs to the eelpout family. It lives on the bottom, from the Gulf of St. Lawrence to Delaware. The Ocean Pout's dorsal, tail, and anal fins are continuous, except for a curious section of *short spines* on the upper side, just before the tail. Like other eelpouts, this fish has a large head and tiny, flaplike pelvic fins. (Some eelpouts have no pelvic fins at all.) The Ocean Pout is an excellent food fish, but is not yet popular. This may be due to its unattractive appearance.

POLLACK

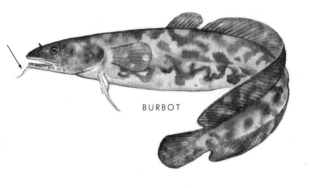

BURBOT

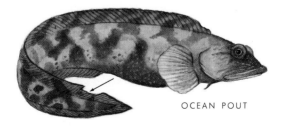

OCEAN POUT

Flyingfishes and Relatives

Despite their name, the flyingfishes cannot fly. However, they can launch themselves from the surface of the sea and glide on their enlarged, *winglike pectoral fins*. A flyingfish is unmistakable. Besides its pectoral "wings," it has a small mouth, a slender body, dorsal and anal fins set far back, and a deeply forked tail with a *lower lobe* that is *longer* than the upper lobe. This unusual tail shape helps to launch the flyingfish into the air. People usually encounter flyingfishes when the fishes land, by accident, in boats. Twenty-three species of flyingfishes are found in the open ocean off both coasts. The California Flyingfish, pictured here, reaches a length of 1½ ft. and ranges from Oregon to Baja California.

HALFBEAKS AND OTHERS

HALFBEAK   To 11 in.
The Halfbeak is a non-gliding member of the flyingfish family. Its body plan is very similar to that of a flyingfish, but it has relatively small pectoral fins and a *long lower beak*, tipped in yellowish red. This peculiar mouth is adapted for surface feeding. The Halfbeak is found skittering at the surface in nearshore waters on both coasts. In the Atlantic, it ranges from Maine to Argentina; in the Pacific, it is found from San Diego to Peru.

ATLANTIC NEEDLEFISH   To 2 ft.
The close relationship of the needlefish family to the flyingfish and halfbeak family is illustrated by the similar arrangement of fins. The Atlantic Needlefish is very long and thin. Both its upper and lower jaws form a *long beak* filled with needle-sharp teeth. It is found in small schools and feeds at night in coastal marine waters and streams, from Maine to Brazil.

BROOK SILVERSIDE   To 4 in.
Found in quiet, clear water throughout the Mississippi River system, this little surface-feeding fish has a *pointed beak*. Many other silversides inhabit salt water. See p. 60.

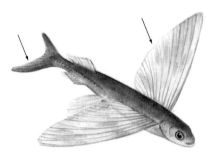

FLYINGFISH

HALFBEAK

ATLANTIC NEEDLEFISH

BROOK SILVERSIDE

CALIFORNIA GRUNION   To 7½ in.

This little Pacific silverside is famous for its unusual spawning technique. From March to September, adult Grunions come onto the beach during the nights of the highest tides, about 4 days after the full moon or new moon. The female buries her eggs in a hole in the wet sand, where they are fertilized by the male. About 2 weeks later, at the next extra-high tide, the eggs hatch. Spawning grunion may be collected by hand only. Found from San Francisco to Baja California, the California Grunion has 2 *small dorsal fins* and a *long anal fin.*

MOSQUITOFISH   To 2½ in.

The Mosquitofish is plainly colored, with a dark bar through the eye. The female (shown) is larger than the male and gives birth to live young. The natural range of the Mosquitofish stretches from New Jersey to central Mexico. Because of its reputation as a voracious predator of mosquito larvae, this fish has been introduced throughout the world. Unfortunately, the Mosquitofish often outcompetes and preys upon native fish species, causing their decline. Thoughtlessly introducing fishes outside their native ranges is almost always a mistake.

KILLIFISHES

This is a large family of small fishes found in fresh and salt water. All have a single dorsal fin and an unforked tail. Males are often colorful enough to be popular in the home aquarium trade.

DESERT PUPFISH   To 2½ in.

The 13 pupfish species of the Southwest have some of the most restricted ranges of any animals — some are found in only a single small spring. The Desert Pupfish inhabits desert springs and streams in a small area of southern California and Arizona and northern Mexico. The breeding male is *iridescent blue* with irregular *dusky bars.* The female is deeper-bodied than the male.

CALIFORNIA GRUNION

female

MOSQUITOFISH

breeding male

DESERT PUPFISH

KILLIFISHES, *continued*

MUMMICHOG   To 5 in.
The Mummichog is a hardy creature of the intertidal zone. It is nearly always found in salt marshes, tidal creeks, and in the tidal areas of estuaries and river mouths, from the Gulf of St. Lawrence to northern Florida. The Mummichog is somewhat more slender than other killifishes, with dark and silver *side bars*. The male's pattern becomes more vivid during the summer spawning season.

SHEEPSHEAD MINNOW   To 3 in.
Often found with the Mummichog (see above), this little killifish can be distinguished by its deep body and squared-off tail fin with a *black edge.* From Cape Cod to the Caribbean and the Gulf of Mexico, the Sheepshead is found in tidal areas and, occasionally, fresh water.

DIAMOND KILLIFISH   To 2 in.
The Diamond Killifish is quite common in intertidal areas such as salt marshes, mangrove swamps, and tidepools along the Gulf Coast from southern Florida to southern Texas. It is very attractive, with its deep body and dozen or so vertical *pearly bands.* The Diamond Killifish takes its name from the shape of its body.

GOLDEN TOPMINNOW   To 3 in.
This freshwater killifish is found in slow, warm water with abundant plant life in the Deep South, from coastal South Carolina to eastern Texas. It has a slender body covered with *spots*, which are red on the male (shown here) and golden on the female. From March to August, Golden Topminnow females deposit their eggs in dense vegetation.

MUMMICHOG

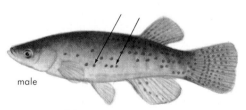

SHEEPSHEAD MINNOW

DIAMOND KILLIFISH

GOLDEN TOPMINNOW

Seahorses and Relatives

THREESPINE STICKLEBACK To 4 in.

This wide-ranging little fish is found in both fresh and salt water from Hudson Bay to Chesapeake Bay in the East, and from the Bering Sea to Baja California in the West. It is also found in Europe and Asia. Its body is shaped like a torpedo and is armed with the *3 dorsal spines* that give the fish its name. The male weaves a nest of vegetation and does an elaborate "dance" to lure the female to lay her eggs there. For several weeks the male stays with the nest, guarding the eggs and developing young.

TRUMPETFISH To 2½ ft.

This long, thin fish hovers vertically among long, fingerlike corals, on shallow reefs from southern Florida to Brazil. This hides the fish from its predators and prey alike. There are *10 isolated spines* before its dorsal fin. The Trumpetfish feeds by sucking small shrimps and fishes into its long snout.

PIPEFISHES

There are 2 varieties of pipefishes — the long, thin pipefish species and the curled seahorses. Both forms have bodies encased in bony rings and brood their young in pouches.

BAY PIPEFISH To 14 in.

The Bay Pipefish is well adapted to hide among eelgrass beds. A very thin fish with a *long snout*, it is green to mottled brown, depending on the color of its habitat. The Bay Pipefish has no pelvic fins. It lives in bays from southern Alaska to Baja California.

LINED SEAHORSE To 6 in.

Like all seahorses, the Lined swims vertically, with its head facing forward. The curled, prehensile tail lacks a tail fin. This seahorse is found among vegetation, from Nova Scotia to Argentina. Its body coloration is quite variable, depending on its habitat: it can be black, pale, red, or gray, plain or marked. Lined Seahorses that live in sargassum weed often are covered with fleshy tabs.

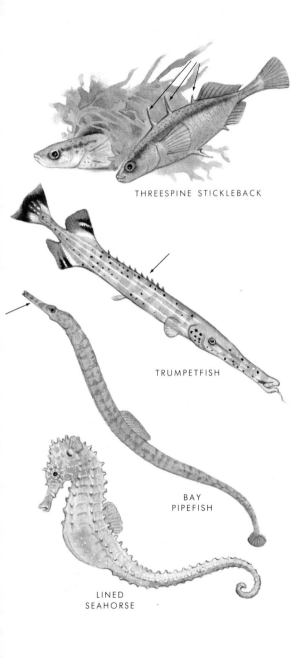

THREESPINE STICKLEBACK

TRUMPETFISH

BAY
PIPEFISH

LINED
SEAHORSE

Perches and Relatives

SNOOK   To 4½ ft.

Like all members of its family, the Snook is a long, even-colored fish. Its body is olive-green to pale green. From behind the long, tapered head, a *thin, black lateral line* runs all the way *to the end* of the tail fin. The Snook's fins are pale to dark. This popular Atlantic sport fish is found in warm inshore waters from South Carolina and Texas to Brazil. Be careful of the sharp edge of the gill cover.

TEMPERATE BASSES

As the name implies, members of the temperate bass family live throughout the temperate zones. They inhabit both fresh and coastal marine waters and are often found in the brackish water of estuaries and river mouths. Most have a *forked tail* and *only 2 spines* on the gill cover.

WHITE PERCH   To 19 in.

A *pale, silvery fish* with a greenish gray back. The White Perch can be found in the brackish water of bays and estuaries and the fresh water of rivers and lakes from the Canadian maritimes to the Carolinas. Although the range of this important game fish has been extended to Lake Erie, its overall numbers have declined.

WHITE BASS   To 1½ ft.

An important sport fish, found in clear lakes, reservoirs, and large streams throughout the middle of North America. This bass is silvery, with 6–9 thin dark stripes. It hunts in schools for fish and insects.

STRIPED BASS   To 6 ft.

The "Striper" is *silvery, with 6–9 black stripes* on the sides. It lives from the St. Lawrence River to northern Florida, and in the Gulf of Mexico from Louisiana to Florida. This very popular but threatened game fish spawns in rivers and estuaries. Pollution of its spawning areas, such as Chesapeake Bay and the Hudson River, is causing its decline.

SNOOK

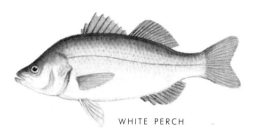

WHITE PERCH

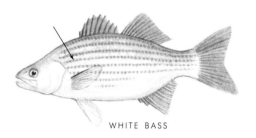

WHITE BASS

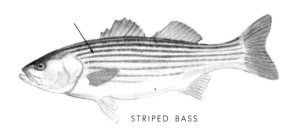

STRIPED BASS

SEA BASSES

This diverse family of fishes ranges in size from 4 in. to 9 ft. The dorsal fins are usually connected and there are usually 3 spines on the gill cover. Some sea basses routinely change sex as they grow. The young ones are female and the older ones male.

GIANT SEA BASS   To 7½ ft.

This heavy bass changes color and pattern as it grows. The juvenile is *red with black spots*, the older fish is *whitish with black spots*, and the gigantic adult is uniformly dark. This bass can be found from Humboldt Bay, California, to the Gulf of California, over rocky bottoms and kelp beds. Its numbers are declining, so California law requires that you release it if you catch it.

RED GROUPER   To 2½ ft.

With dark red-brown sides interrupted by several pale patches, this is a handsome, medium-sized grouper. *Black borders* on the *soft dorsal, tail, and anal fins* complete the picture. This is an important commercial food fish, especially in Mexico. It is found in water 80–400 ft. deep over rocky reefs, from Massachusetts to Brazil.

KELP BASS   To 2 ft.

For a sea bass, this fish is rather elongated, with a pointed head. The Kelp Bass has a white belly and greenish brown sides with *white blotches* above the lateral line. It is found from Oregon to Baja California. Up to a million of these delicious fish are taken every year in southern California alone.

BLACK SEA BASS   To 2 ft.

This dark sea bass has handsome bars above its lateral line which are formed by the light centers of its scales. The spines of its 1st dorsal fin sport *unusual fleshy flaps*. The rounded tail fin often has elongated upper rays. Males have white patches on the head and fin edges. Anglers catch this fish around piers and wrecks, from Maine to Florida and in the Gulf of Mexico.

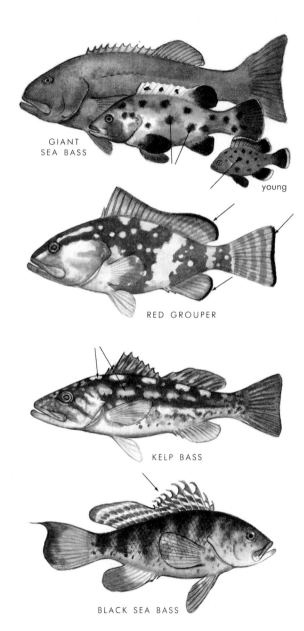

GIANT SEA BASS

young

RED GROUPER

KELP BASS

BLACK SEA BASS

SUNFISHES

This family includes many of North America's favorite freshwater sport fishes. Whether deep-bodied or elongate, all have connected dorsal fins and slightly forked tails. Most sunfishes protect their eggs in nests. See also p. 72.

GREEN SUNFISH To 10 in.

This olive to yellow-green fish is more slender than the Bluegill or Pumpkinseed, with a *mouth extending to* the area *below the middle of the eye.* Native to ponds and slow streams from the southern Great Lakes through the Mississippi River basin, the Green Sunfish has been widely introduced elsewhere. Its rapid colonizing ability has caused the decline of other fishes in new territories.

PUMPKINSEED To 10 in.

The very pretty Pumpkinseed is mottled gold, orange, and green. The distinctive *flap, or "ear,"* on the gill cover is *black, edged with white above and below,* and *orange at the rear.* Found between Georgia and southern Canada, this sunfish prefers cool, shallow water with little current and much plant life. A Pumpkinseed is often a young angler's first catch.

BLUEGILL To 12 in.

Colored a dark olive mottled with light green, Bluegills often show *dark side bars.* There is also a *black ear flap* and often a dark area on the 2nd dorsal fin. Native from southern Canada to the Gulf of Mexico, this sunfish has been widely introduced elsewhere.

LONGEAR SUNFISH To 9 in.

True to its name, the Longear has an *ear flap* that is quite long. Green mottled with blue on the sides, this sunfish has a reddish or yellowish belly. The Longear prefers a little faster current than other sunfishes. It is a popular little sport fish throughout its natural range, from the Great Lakes through the Mississippi River system.

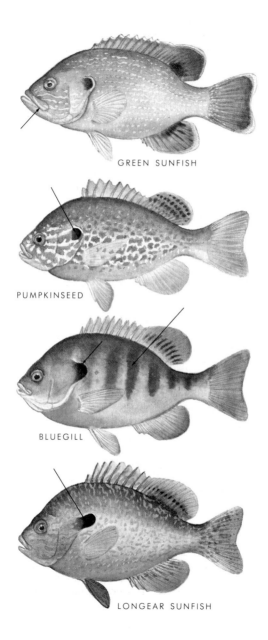

GREEN SUNFISH

PUMPKINSEED

BLUEGILL

LONGEAR SUNFISH

SUNFISHES, *continued*

BLACK CRAPPIE   To 16 in.

Together with its close relative, the White Crappie, this is the largest of the deep-bodied sunfishes. Its even green color (darker on the back) is enhanced by a mottling of dark green to black. The Crappie's dorsal, anal, and tail fins bear *many spots.* It has a *larger mouth* than the Bluegill and a *longer head,* which is *slightly indented between the eyes.* An excellent food fish, it has been introduced well outside its original range — the U.S. and southern Canada east of the Rockies.

LARGEMOUTH BASS   To 2 ft., 8 in.

This bass and the Smallmouth and Spotted basses are actually elongated sunfishes. The Largemouth Bass prefers quiet, clear streams, lakes, and reservoirs with plenty of vegetation near the banks where its young can hide. In years of low water, most young fail to survive. The Largemouth is dark green to greenish yellow, with a *dark, mottled side stripe.* It does have a *large mouth that extends* past the eye. A favorite sport fish, the Largemouth has been widely introduced, with disastrous results for the native fish. Its original range was confined to the Great Lakes region, the Mississippi River system, and most of the South.

SMALLMOUTH BASS   To 2 ft.

This greenish yellow bass has *mottled dark side bars.* The mouth extends to a point *below* the eye but *not beyond it.* The Smallmouth thrives in swifter currents than the Largemouth. When introduced together into reservoirs, the Smallmouth stays nearer the upper end. It is a popular game fish from southern Canada to the central U.S.

SPOTTED BASS   To 2 ft.

This fish is olive to yellow-green, with an *irregular side stripe of dark blotches.* Sometimes confused with the Largemouth, the Spotted Bass has a *smaller mouth* and a *spot at the base of the tail fin.* It is native to the Mississippi River system.

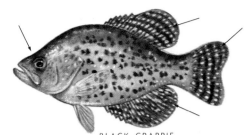

BLACK CRAPPIE

LARGEMOUTH BASS

SMALLMOUTH BASS

SPOTTED BASS

PERCHES

Perches range in size from the tiny darters to the mighty Walleye. They are slender fishes with clearly separate dorsal fins. Ninety percent of the species in this family live in North American fresh waters. It almost seems that every stream east of the Rockies has its unique, colorful darter.

JOHNNY DARTER   To 2½ in.

The Johnny is a slender, yellow to amber darter. The *dark zigzag line* down its side is often broken up into V, W, or X marks. The rows of fin spots become dusky in the breeding male. Like all darters, this fish has no swim bladder; the resulting lack of buoyancy allows the fish to lie on the bottom. It usually lies in gravel beds near the shallow rapids of clear streams. The Johnny ranges from Hudson Bay to the upper Mississippi — the widest range of any darter.

RAINBOW DARTER   To 3 in.

Longer and thicker than the Johnny, the Rainbow is truly a *rainbow of blues, greens, and reds.* This darter lives near rapids in clear streams from the southern Great Lakes through the Mississippi River system. It is very sensitive to pollution, mud, and silt.

YELLOW PERCH   To 15 in.

This common perch is a striking greenish gold with *black bars* and (in the breeding season) orange lower fins. Found in clear, open areas of streams, lakes, and reservoirs, the Yellow Perch feeds in the shallows at dawn and dusk — good times to fish for it. It ranges from central Canada to the upper Mississippi River system.

WALLEYE   To 3 ft., 5 in.

A very popular, large sport fish, found in deep water throughout much of central Canada and the U.S. The Walleye uses its large, reflective eyes to hunt at dawn and dusk. This perch has *dusky, saddle-like patches* on its body. There is a distinctive *white tip* on the lower lobe of the tail fin.

JOHNNY DARTER

RAINBOW DARTER

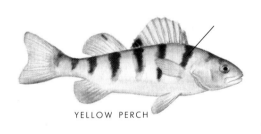

YELLOW PERCH

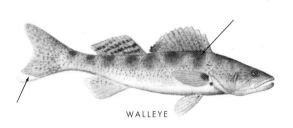

WALLEYE

MORE PERCH RELATIVES

OCEAN WHITEFISH   To 3 ft., 4 in.
This Pacific member of the tilefish family is
found in rather deep water over soft bottoms, from Vancouver Island to Peru. Somewhat streamlined, with a blunt head, this
fish has a *single long dorsal fin* and a
shorter, blue-striped anal fin. The Ocean
Whitefish fights when hooked and tastes
delicious — an ideal game fish.

BLUEFISH   To 3½ ft.
The Bluefish is the only North American
member of its family. It is an elongate, *blue-
gray to silvery* fish, with a big head and a
big mouth filled with big, sharp teeth. Its
2nd dorsal and anal fins are covered with
small scales. Schools of hungry Bluefish
sometimes enter the surf, slicing at anything in the water, including unwary bath-
ers. Throughout its range (Nova Scotia to
Argentina) the Bluefish is a prized sport
fish. Its fighting behavior when hooked is
true to its scientific name: *saltatrix*, "the
leaper."

COBIA   To 6 ft., 7 in.
The Cobia is the only member of its family.
It is dark brown above, with a dark side
stripe and a pale belly. Behind its distinctive flattened head is a 1st dorsal fin com-
posed of *7–9 very short, unconnected
spines* and a long 2nd dorsal fin with a high
peak in front. The Cobia prefers the open
ocean and the vicinity of reefs and islands
from New York to Argentina. It often basks
at the surface.

SHARKSUCKER   To 3 ft.
Like other remoras, the Sharksucker has an
unusual *sucking disk on top of its head.*
This disk (actually a highly modified 1st
dorsal fin) allows the fish to cling harmlessly
to large animals such as whales, turtles,
sharks, and other large fish. This remora
darts away from its host to catch small fish
and scavenge scraps of food. It is a dark fish
with a *white belly* and a *dark, white-edged
stripe* from front to back. Sharksuckers live
in open water from Nova Scotia to Brazil.

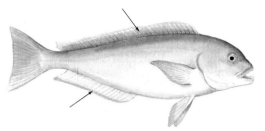

OCEAN WHITEFISH

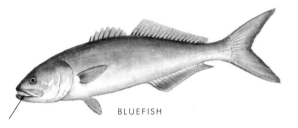

BLUEFISH

COBIA

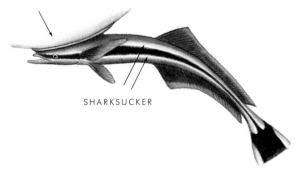

SHARKSUCKER

JACKS

The members of this large family vary in shape from deep-bodied to long and slender. In many jacks, the 2nd dorsal and anal fins seem like mirror images. These fast, silvery predators usually travel in schools.

CREVALLE JACK
To 3 ft., 4 in.

This jack is compressed, with a high, rounded profile and a *large mouth.* It is a popular, fighting sport fish on both coasts (Atlantic: Nova Scotia to Uruguay; Pacific: San Diego to South America). The Crevalle Jack resembles the Florida Pompano, a close relative found only in the Atlantic, but can be distinguished by its larger mouth. It sports black areas on its gill cover and pectoral fins.

LOOKDOWN
To 16 in.

The Lookdown is *very compressed* ("dishlike"), with a *high forehead* and a *straight-line profile.* It is silvery all over, and the first rays of its anal and 2nd dorsal fins are very long. When very young, the Lookdown (like other jacks) has very long, ribbonlike appendages on its fins. Found in warm Atlantic waters from New England to South America, it prefers muddy or sandy bottoms.

GREATER AMBERJACK
To 5 ft.

This large, powerful jack has a characteristic *brown or olive stripe* running from the snout *through the eye,* to the 1st dorsal fin. The body is a pale brown, sometimes with a yellowish side stripe. The Amberjack is a popular sport fish of the open ocean, from New England to Brazil.

YELLOWTAIL
To 5 ft.

Shaped like the Amberjack, this Pacific fish has *yellow fins* as well as a *yellow stripe.* From British Columbia to Chile, it seeks out warmer water. Variable water temperatures account for a variable catch in California; when the water cools, the Yellowtail population migrates south.

CREVALLE JACK

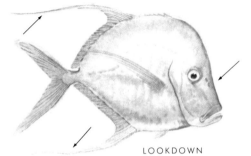

LOOKDOWN

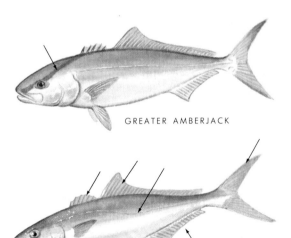

GREATER AMBERJACK

YELLOWTAIL

MORE PERCH RELATIVES

DOLPHIN
To 6 ft.

This fish is not, of course, related to the small toothed whales that are also called dolphins. The unique profile of this fish (*high forehead, single long dorsal fin, deeply forked tail*) tells of great speed. The Dolphin's gorgeous *iridescent blue, green, and yellow colors* disappear after death. Found in open water from Nova Scotia to Brazil, the Dolphin is highly prized as food (called "mahi-mahi" on the menu) by humans as well as by most ocean predators. That is why it needs to swim so fast.

SNAPPERS

This family of medium to large fishes includes many important commercial and sport species. Most are bottom-feeding predators, active at dawn and dusk.

SCHOOLMASTER
To 2 ft.

This grayish fish always has attractive *yellow fins* and *8 pale bars* on its sides. The *blue stripe below the eye* is usually solid in young Schoolmasters but broken in adults. From New England to Brazil, the Schoolmaster is found inshore, among rocks, turtle grass, mangroves, and in tidepools. However, it is most common on coral reefs.

RED SNAPPER
To 2½ ft.

The *bright red body, fins and eye* of this fish are a clue that it lives in deep water. In the dim, blue light of the depths, red fish appear black and can hide from their prey. The Red Snapper seems to prefer deep reefs and rocks throughout its range — North Carolina to Florida and the Gulf of Mexico. Artificial reefs have been built in the Gulf to attract this snapper for sport fishing.

GRAY SNAPPER
To 2½ ft.

A *red edge* to the 1st dorsal fin relieves the uniform gray with reddish tones of the Gray Snapper. Like many other subtropical fishes, the Gray Snapper spends its early life sheltered in mangrove swamps. This excellent food fish is found in warm inshore waters from New England to Brazil.

DOLPHIN

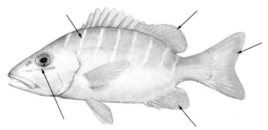

SCHOOLMASTER

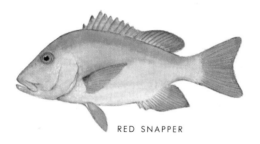

RED SNAPPER

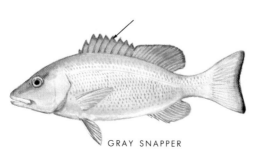

GRAY SNAPPER

MORE PERCH RELATIVES

SPOTFIN MOJARRA   To 8 in.

The most remarkable feature of all mojarras, including the Spotfin, is a mouth with *jaws that can be extended* to form a short, downward-pointing tube. Mojarras use this tube-like mouth to suck up worms and other invertebrates from sandy bottoms. The slender Spotfin has *one or more dark spots* on its 1st dorsal fin. It is found from New Jersey to Brazil, but not on coral reefs.

WHITE GRUNT   To 18 in.

The grunt family gets its name from the grunting sound the fishes make by grinding together special teeth. Like other grunts (such as the Porkfish and French Grunt), the White is often displayed in public aquaria. Its striking *pattern of bronze and blue stripes fades* above the lateral line. Found from Maryland to Brazil, this fish lives over sand and grass flats and near reefs.

SEA CHUBS

This family of oval fishes is found on both coasts. They have small mouths, used primarily for nibbling algae. Nicknamed "rudderfishes," sea chubs often follow ships.

OPALEYE   To 2 ft., 2 in.

The beautiful *blue eyes* give the Opaleye its name. Usually there are *2 white or yellowish spots* on the side. Found from San Francisco to Baja California, the Opaleye is a popular and spirited game fish. It feeds on algae and eelgrass, but the microscopic animals growing on the plants are also thought to be an important part of its diet.

BERMUDA CHUB   To 20 in.

This Atlantic sea chub ranges from Cape Cod to Brazil, including the Gulf of Mexico, the Caribbean, and (not surprisingly) Bermuda. It is also found across the Atlantic, near Europe and Africa. The *pale yellow side stripes* distinguish the Bermuda Chub from the Yellow Chub. Neither of these algae-eaters is highly prized as food.

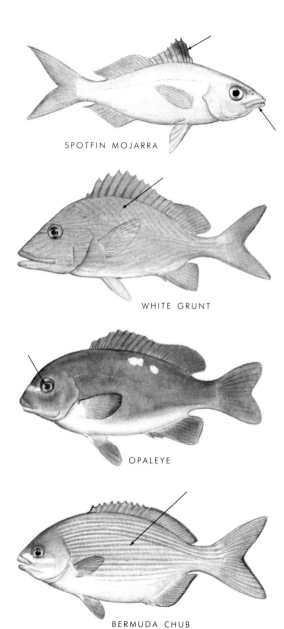

SPOTFIN MOJARRA

WHITE GRUNT

OPALEYE

BERMUDA CHUB

PORGIES

Porgies roam in groups over hard or soft bottoms, picking small invertebrates from their hiding places. These fishes have a *small mouth* with a *tooth pattern* that is unusual for fishes — incisorlike teeth in the front and molarlike teeth in the rear. Porgies have *large eyes* with *slitlike nostrils in front*.

JOLTHEAD PORGY   To 2 ft.

This *large-headed* porgy lives along coasts and over reefs, from Rhode Island to Brazil. It picks up hard invertebrates such as sea urchins with its sharp front teeth and crushes them with its hard molars. Under the eye is a blue line. Like other porgies, the Jolthead has a *single long dorsal fin* and a *forked tail*.

PINFISH   To 15 in.

This is a small porgy with *thin yellow stripes* and a *dark spot* on the shoulder, *centered on the lateral line*. It can be distinguished from the similar Sea Bream (not shown), whose dark spot lies *below* the lateral line. The Pinfish lives in shallow water, from Massachusetts to the Yucatán Peninsula of Mexico. Because of its small size, it is not an important food fish.

SHEEPSHEAD   To 3 ft.

The Sheepshead has *flat front teeth* that occasionally protude a little beyond its lips, giving it a vaguely sheeplike appearance. Its sides are marked by *several dark bars*. The Sheepshead is found in the shallow, muddy waters of bays and estuaries from New England to Brazil, although it is absent from the Caribbean. Anglers should be wary of the strong, sharp spines in front of the dorsal and anal fins.

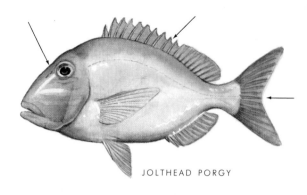

JOLTHEAD PORGY

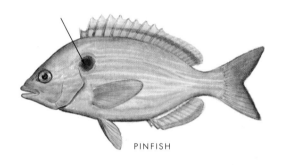

PINFISH

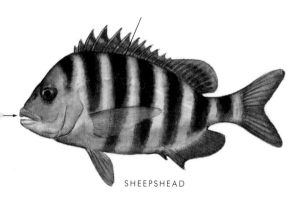

SHEEPSHEAD

MORE PERCH RELATIVES

TRIPLETAIL   To 3½ ft.

Despite its name, the Tripletail has but one
tail. Its 2nd dorsal and anal *fins extend so
far back*, however, that the *impression of 3
tails* is understandable. This fish is often
seen lying on its side at the surface. This
habit and its mottled pattern help it to
mimic dead leaves or bark. This excellent
food fish is found from the Carolinas to
Argentina, either in the open ocean or
inshore near pilings and buoys. The young
are seen as far north as Cape Cod.

DRUMS

Many members of this family are named for
the sounds they make: croakers croak and
drums make a drumming sound. Most of
these fishes probe the bottom with sensitive
chin barbels, searching for shrimp and
other invertebrate prey. Many drums are
delicious food fishes.

WHITE SEABASS   To 5 ft.

The White Seabass is not white and is not a
true sea bass (see p. 68); it is a blue-gray to
silvery drum. Unlike most drums, it has *no
chin barbels*; it has no need for them
because it feeds on fishes and squids in
midwater. There is a black spot at the base
of each pectoral fin. The White Seabass is
found in inshore waters from southern
Alaska to Baja California.

SPOTTED SEA TROUT   To 3 ft.

Found from New York to Florida and in the
Gulf of Mexico, the Spotted Sea Trout is
prized by anglers. Its sides, 2nd dorsal fin,
and tail fin are *peppered with bold, dotlike
spots*. The sea trouts, which are not related
to the true trouts (see p. 30), live over shallow sand flats.

WEAKFISH   To 3 ft.

This fish is similar to the Spotted Sea Trout
but has *smaller spots* that *often form diagonal streaks*. It is popular with anglers
throughout its range (Nova Scotia to Florida) but, without careful handling, the hook
can easily tear from the mouth. This ten-
dency gives the fish its name.

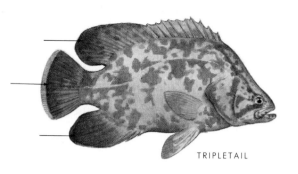

TRIPLETAIL

WHITE SEABASS

SPOTTED SEATROUT

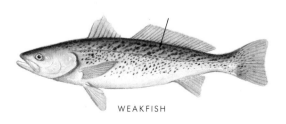

WEAKFISH

DRUMS AND OTHERS

FRESHWATER DRUM   To 3 ft.

Our only drum that lives in fresh water. This *robust fish* with *2 anal-fin spines* is found throughout central North America, from southern Canada to Mexico. It inhabits deep pools of streams and lakes, where it eats snails, insect larvae, and other invertebrates. Its "earstones" — stony growths from the inner ear that help the fish keep its balance — are kept by anglers as lucky charms.

SOUTHERN KINGFISH   To 1½ ft.

This slender drum, like the related Northern and Gulf kingfishes, can be caught by surf-casting. The Southern Kingfish lives from New York to northern Florida and in the Gulf of Mexico. A *single chin barbel* and *7–8 dark, broad diagonal bands* identify it.

ATLANTIC CROAKER   To 2 ft.

Rows of *small spots form diagonal lines* on the sides of this croaker. *Very small chin barbels* can be found under the lower jaw. This fish lives from Massachusetts to Mexico but is rare in southern Florida. Croakers, like frogs and birds, tend to vocalize ("croak") at dawn and dusk.

RED DRUM   To 5 ft.

This is the main ingredient in the Cajun dish called "blackened redfish." The Red Drum is very popular with surfcasters, especially during its spring and fall migrations. Found from Massachusetts to Mexico, it is most abundant along the Gulf Coast. The Red Drum has a characteristic *dark spot just before* its tail fin. It has *no chin barbels*.

RED GOATFISH   To 10 in.

Like all members of the goatfish family, the Red has 2 *clearly separate dorsal fins* and 2 *long chin barbels*, which help it probe for hidden worms or shrimps. It lives over muddy bottoms near the coast, from New England to South America. The Red Goatfish is blotchy, with *2 reddish or yellowish side stripes*.

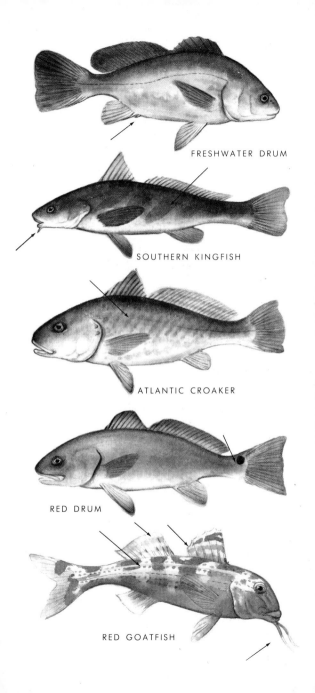

FRESHWATER DRUM

SOUTHERN KINGFISH

ATLANTIC CROAKER

RED DRUM

RED GOATFISH

MORE PERCH RELATIVES

ATLANTIC SPADEFISH   To 3 ft.

Most members of the spadefish family are
tropical, but some, like the Atlantic Spadefish, also inhabit warm-temperate waters.
This fish certainly looks like a tropical fish,
with its *very deep, compressed body; long
2nd dorsal and anal fins;* and *striking
dark bars.* The Atlantic Spadefish can be
found near rocks and reefs (either natural
or artificial) from New England to Brazil. It
feeds on small shellfish and is taken by
spearfishers in the Caribbean. Unlike the
butterflyfishes (see below), the spadefishes
have 2 clearly separate dorsal fins.

FOUREYE BUTTERFLYFISH   To 6 in.

This is the most common butterflyfish. Like
other members of the family, it is a colorful,
compressed fish with a tiny mouth that is
just right for picking worms and other
small prey out of holes and cracks. The
Foureye is found from Massachusetts to
Brazil, on rocks and coral reefs. The distinctive *white-ringed black dot* on its rear
serves to confuse predators about which
end is which. Young Foureyes (not shown)
have another spot on the 2nd dorsal fin.
The 2 eyespots of the young could serve to
startle predators, as do the eyespots of some
moths.

QUEEN ANGELFISH   To 15 in.

The angelfishes are very closely related to
the butterflyfishes. This is easy to under-
stand; both families consist of colorful,
compressed fishes with continuous dorsal
fins and a small mouth. Angelfishes, such
as the Queen Angelfish, differ in having a
blunter snout and spines on the gill cover.
The Queen is certainly regal in appearance,
with its long, graceful fins and beautiful
mixture of blue, orange, and yellow colors.
There is even a *"crown" above its eyes* — a
striking *black spot ringed in blue.* This
angelfish is found on reefs·from Florida to
Brazil. The Queen Angelfish and the Foureye Butterflyfish are often seen in both public and home aquaria.

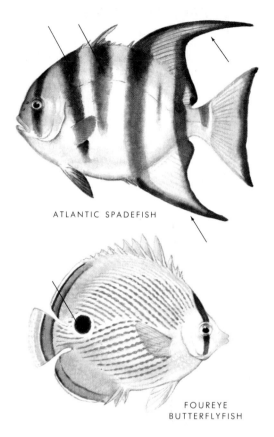

ATLANTIC SPADEFISH

FOUREYE
BUTTERFLYFISH

QUEEN ANGELFISH

MORE PERCH RELATIVES

REDTAIL SURFPERCH   To 16 in.

Most surfperches (except for one freshwater
species from the Sacramento River) live in
salt water in the Pacific. True to its name,
this surfperch hunts in the surf for small,
sand-dwelling invertebrates. Like all members of its family, the Redtail Surfperch is a
livebearer. The female not only retains her
eggs in her body, but actually nourishes the
developing young with her body fluids
before giving birth. The Redtail Surfperch
ranges from Vancouver Island to Monterey
Bay, California. Not surprisingly, the Redtail Surfperch has a *reddish tail.*

DAMSELFISHES

This is a large family of small, colorful fishes
that live mainly in tropical waters. They
have a compressed body, a small mouth,
and *only one nostril on each side.* In most
species the males guard the eggs, which are
stuck to rocks or coral skeletons. Many
damselfishes are popular but aggressive
fishes in aquaria.

SERGEANT MAJOR   To 7 in.

The Sergeant Major's *5 dark bars* reminded
those who named it of military insignia.
This damselfish is most abundant on Caribbean reefs but is occasionally found as far
north as Rhode Island and as far south as
Uruguay. The Sergeant Major is often found
around pilings and sunken ships. It feeds
on small invertebrates and on algae.

GARIBALDI   To 14 in.

As with many bright tropical fishes, the
color pattern of the young Garibaldi differs
from that of the adult. It starts out with
striking blue markings but, at a length of
about 2½ in., it begins to assume the *bright
orange* adult coloration. This beautiful resi-
dent of Pacific kelp beds lives from Monterey
Bay, California, to Baja California. Divers
and aquarists often remark on its noisy
clicking, especially at mealtime. Taking of
the Garibaldi is strictly prohibited in California.

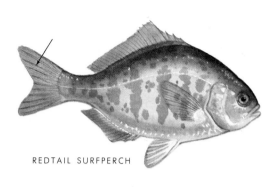

REDTAIL SURFPERCH

SERGEANT MAJOR

GARIBALDI

young

WRASSES

Wrasses range from tiny to huge. Most of them have a small mouth, thick lips, long canine teeth, and a single dorsal fin. Many wrasses are sex-changers, starting as females and growing into males. Males and females often have very different color patterns.

BLUEHEAD   To 7 in.

This tropical fish (found in southern Florida, the Caribbean, the Gulf of Mexico, and Bermuda) comes in 3 sexes: female, male, and supermale! The male and the supermale are really the same sex but differ in appearance and behavior. Male and female Blueheads spawn in large groups, while supermales pair with single females. Juveniles, females, and males are *yellow, with a black spot on the dorsal fin;* in supermales *2 broad black bands* separate the *blue head* from the *greenish yellow rear.*

TAUTOG   To 3 ft.

The Tautog is a large northern wrasse found from Nova Scotia to South Carolina. It feeds on mussels and other hard shellfish, crushing them with its massive teeth. The body is *mottled* in females and young tautogs; large males have a *white chin.* The *scaleless gill cover* has a *velvety feel.* The Tautog is a good food fish.

CUNNER   To 1 ft.

This blotchy wrasse is very variable in color. It can be distinguished from the Tautog by its *more pointed snout* and its *scaly gill cover.* The Cunner is often caught by anglers around rocks, pilings, and wharves, from Newfoundland to New Jersey.

CALIFORNIA SHEEPHEAD   To 3 ft.

This wrasse is found in kelp beds and reefs, from Monterey Bay, California, to Baja California. It feeds on invertebrates. Males are *black* with a *brick-red middle,* females are reddish brown, and juveniles brick-red. Females become males at 7–8 years. This fish is popular with anglers.

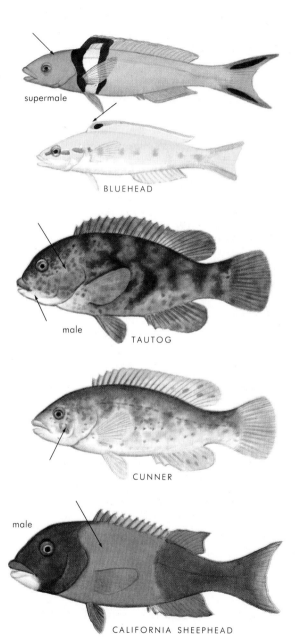

supermale

BLUEHEAD

male

TAUTOG

CUNNER

male

CALIFORNIA SHEEPHEAD

MORE PERCH RELATIVES

QUEEN PARROTFISH   To 2 ft.

This parrotfish is found on coral reefs, from
southern Florida to Colombia. The parrotfishes are closely related to the wrasses. The
main difference is the teeth: parrotfishes
have *teeth fused into a parrotlike beak* that
is used to crunch through coral and other
hard material. When the Queen Parrotfish's
mouth is closed, the *upper beak fits over
the lower one*. Like the wrasses, many parrotfishes can change their sex; there are different color patterns for the sexes. The
female Queen Parrotfish is *brown*, with a
broad, whitish side stripe. The male is
blue-green, with *wavy, yellow and green
stripes on the head*.

STRIPED MULLET   To 1½ ft.

The Striped Mullet lives in large schools on
both coasts, over shallow, muddy bottoms.
It is an important commercial fish. In the
Atlantic it ranges from New England to Brazil; in the Pacific it is found from San Francisco to Chile. Like all members of the
mullet family, the Striped Mullet has a long,
slender body; a *small, angled mouth*; and *2
short, well-separated dorsal fins*. On its
sides are *several thin stripes*. This mullet
feeds by scooping up mouthfuls of mud. As
the mud passes through its extraordinarily
long gut, the fish digests the tiny plants in
the mud.

GREAT BARRACUDA   To 6 ft.

Barracudas are greatly feared for their
attacks on people, even though these inci-
dents are rather uncommon. Barracudas
are probably more dangerous dead than
alive, because they often contain ciguatera
toxin (see p. 9). Nevertheless, divers should
be wary of these large, fast, toothy predators. The Great Barracuda is found from
Massachusetts to Brazil. Like all barracudas, it is *long and slender*, with *silvery
sides*, a *large head and eyes*, and a *large
mouth full of sharp teeth*. The body shape
and *widely separated dorsal fins* reveal the
surprisingly close relationship between barracudas and mullets.

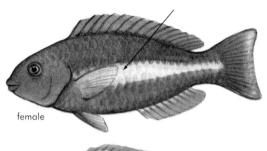

female

male

QUEEN PARROTFISH

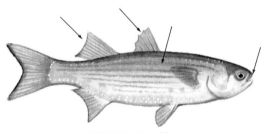

STRIPED MULLET

GREAT BARRACUDA

CLINIDS

Typically, these bottom-dwelling fishes are so small that a species attaining a mere 2 ft. is called the Giant Kelpfish. Clinids are elongated, with long dorsal fins and pelvic fins set very far forward.

GIANT KELPFISH   To 2 ft.

This fish can be *either greenish yellow or ruddy brown with light stripes.* It lives in kelp beds as well as among other sorts of vegetation, from British Columbia to Baja California. This kelpfish has a *pointed snout* with a *lower jaw* that is *longer than the upper one.* Unlike other clinids, the Giant Kelpfish has a *forked tail.*

ONESPOT FRINGEHEAD   To 9 in.

Its name hints that this fish has a *spot* (on the *front of its long dorsal fin*) and a *fringe of growths* (called *cirri*) on its head. From Bodega Bay, California, to Baja California, the Onespot lives in holes in rocky reefs or soft bottoms. Anglers should be careful; it bites when reeled in.

FEATHER BLENNY   To 4 in.

Like the other members of the combtooth blenny family, this fish has many small, closely packed teeth. It has *fleshy cirri over its eyes,* an *upper lip joined to the snout,* and a blotchy pattern. This blenny ranges from New England to Mexico. It spawns in empty shells on oyster reefs.

GOBIES

Most gobies have a suction disk formed from their pelvic fins. This is the largest family of marine fishes.

NAKED GOBY   To 2½ in.

This *brown-barred* goby lives from New York to Texas. It *completely lacks scales.*

BLUEBANDED GOBY   To 2½ in.

Bright red with *electric blue bands,* this common Pacific goby is a popular aquarium fish. It inhabits rocky crevices, from Morro Bay, California, to Baja California.

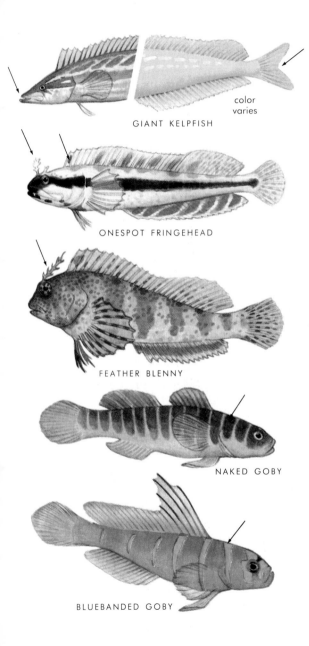

GIANT KELPFISH

color
varies

ONESPOT FRINGEHEAD

FEATHER BLENNY

NAKED GOBY

BLUEBANDED GOBY

GUNNELS

These long, eel-like fishes live in the intertidal zone. They prefer cold water.

PENPOINT GUNNEL To 1½ ft.

This uncommon gunnel *lacks pelvic fins*
and has a *strong spine* on its *anal fin*. The
Penpoint eats small invertebrates in intertidal areas, from Alaska to southern California.

ROCK GUNNEL To 1 ft.

This common Atlantic gunnel has a *dark
bar* running from behind the mouth
through the eye to the dorsal fin, and has a
series of *black spots* along the base of the
dorsal fin. It is sometimes found in tidepools, from Labrador to Delaware.

WOLFFISHES

Like wolves, these fishes can inflict nasty
bites. Members of this family are huge relatives of the blennies (see p. 98); they are
long, with large pectoral fins but no pelvic
fins.

ATLANTIC WOLFFISH To 5 ft.

This large, eel-like fish has *several irregular
side bars*. Be careful of the powerful jaws,
which crush shellfish and starfish. The
Atlantic Wolffish lives from Greenland to
Cape Cod.

WOLF-EEL To 6 ft., 8 in.

Tapering from a *massive head* to a *tiny,
pointed tail*, the Wolf-eel's body is *spotted
dark gray-brown* on a *light background*.
This fish feeds on hard shellfish and sea
urchins from Alaska to southern California.
Divers should be wary of the Wolf-eel's powerful jaws and teeth.

MONKEYFACE PRICKLEBACK To 2½ ft.

Pricklebacks have *long, spiny dorsal fins*
and are kin of blennies. The Monkeyface,
found from Oregon to Baja California, has *2
fleshy humps* on its head. Its East Coast
relative, the Atlantic Warbonnet (not
shown), also has fleshy headgear. It lives in
holes in rocks.

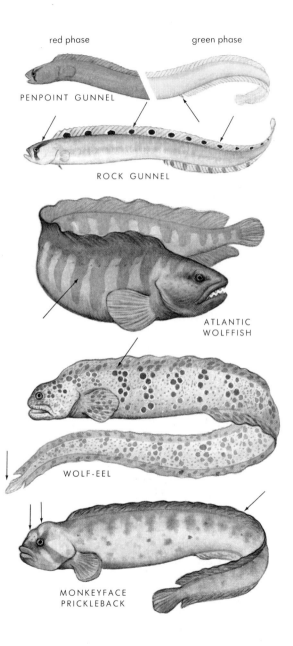

red phase

green phase

PENPOINT GUNNEL

ROCK GUNNEL

ATLANTIC
WOLFFISH

WOLF-EEL

MONKEYFACE
PRICKLEBACK

MACKERELS

With their fusiform (cigar-shaped) bodies and half-moon-shaped tails, mackerels are built for speed. Look for the rows of finlets in front of the tail. Mackerels are also among our most important food fish.

WAHOO   To 6 ft.

This outstanding sport fish has *long, beak-like jaws* and *many dark, wavy bars*. It lives in the open ocean on both coasts and feeds on squid and fish. In the Atlantic it ranges from New York to South America; in the Pacific, from California to South America.

ATLANTIC MACKEREL   To 1 ft., 10 in.

An important commercial fishery depends on this abundant fish, which schools from Newfoundland to Cape Hatteras. Fresh or canned, it is delicious. Its characteristic *wavy bands stop just below the lateral line.*

SKIPJACK TUNA   To 3 ft., 3 in.

This tuna can be identified by its 3–6 *dark side stripes.* Often sought for food or sport, it inhabits both coasts (Atlantic: New England to Argentina; Pacific: Canada to Peru).

ALBACORE   To 5 ft.

Only the Albacore has such a *long, winglike pectoral fin.* This tuna is valued for food and sport on both coasts; its name (*alba* means "white") alludes to its white meat, which is prized for canning. In the Atlantic, this tuna ranges from Nova Scotia to Brazil; in the Pacific, from Alaska to Mexico.

BLUEFIN TUNA   To 10 ft.

This gigantic ocean predator can sometimes be seen leaping from the water in pursuit of its relative, the Mackerel. This tuna has a *short pectoral fin* and *yellow finlets.* Highly prized on both coasts (Atlantic range: Labrador to Brazil; Pacific: Alaska to Peru), record specimens approach 1500 pounds! Fresh Bluefin is especially popular in Japan.

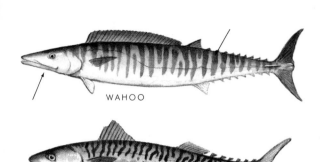

WAHOO

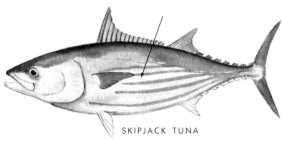

ATLANTIC MACKEREL

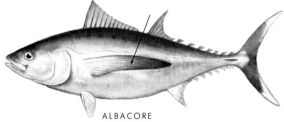

SKIPJACK TUNA

ALBACORE

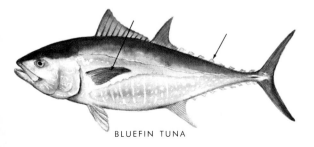

BLUEFIN TUNA

SWORDFISH   To 15 ft.

Despite superficial appearances, the Swordfish is not related to the billfishes (see below); in fact, it is the only member of its family. It does have a *long, swordlike beak*, but its *tall dorsal fin is rigid* and it *completely lacks pectoral fins.* The Swordfish is one of the most sought-after sport and commercial fishes on either coast. It ranges from Nova Scotia to Argentina and from Oregon to Chile.

BILLFISHES

All the members of this family have long, swordlike bills. Their long dorsal fins fold into grooves. They have *well-developed pectoral fins,* but their pelvic fins are reduced to long, thin projections. These fish- and squid-eating predators are among the fastest fishes in the ocean.

SAILFISH   To 10 ft.

The Sailfish has an unmistakable *sail-like dorsal fin, higher in the middle* than at either end. Like many billfishes, it is found on both coasts, from New England to Brazil and from San Diego to Chile. This is a very popular sport fish, especially in warmer waters.

BLUE MARLIN   To 14 ft.

This very large and important sport and food fish lives near the surface of the open ocean. It is one of the few fishes fast enough to prey on the smaller tunas. The Blue is the only large marlin found on both coasts. In the Atlantic it ranges from New England to Uruguay; in the Pacific, from southern California to South America. The Blue Marlin can be recognized by its *side bars,* which are formed by *pale blue spots.*

BUTTERFISH   To 1 ft.

Members of the butterfish family superficially resemble some of the jacks (p. 78). The Butterfish is very compressed, with *mirror-image dorsal and anal fins.* This silvery little fish with *irregular dark spots* is found from Newfoundland to Florida.

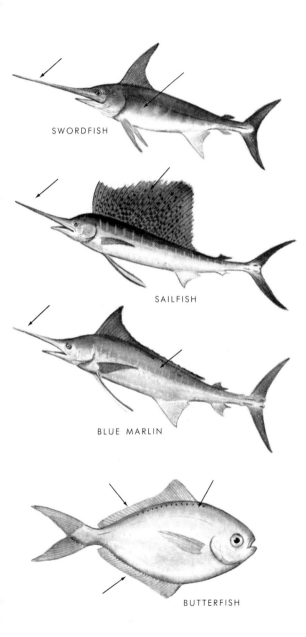

SWORDFISH

SAILFISH

BLUE MARLIN

BUTTERFISH

SCORPIONFISHES

The prickly members of this family include important food species as well as some of the most venomous fishes in the world. The stout spines of the pelvic, dorsal, and anal fins deliver the venom. Most scorpionfishes are bottom-dwellers and bear their young alive rather than laying eggs. Many species from this family live along the Pacific Coast, often in the same area. Scorpionfishes grow very slowly and live long lives. See also p. 108.

BARBFISH   To 8 in.

This very mottled scorpionfish has *2 dark bands on the tail fin* and a broad pectoral fin. Found from Virginia to Brazil, this is the most common scorpionfish in Florida waters. The Barbfish's toxin is among the most potent known, so anglers should be very careful when handling it.

VERMILION ROCKFISH   To 2½ ft.

This large Pacific scorpionfish is a popular sport fish and is good to eat. Anglers should be careful of its stout dorsal and anal spines, however. Though it is not as venomous as some of its smaller relatives, the Vermilion Rockfish can cause painful injuries. It is found from British Columbia to Baja California.

GRASS ROCKFISH   To 1 ft., 10 in.

From Oregon to Baja California, this *heavy-bodied, mottled* fish is one of the most commonly caught scorpionfishes. It lives in shallow water around rocks and jetties. As with other members of this family, the Grass Rockfish should be handled carefully when caught. The careful angler, however, will be rewarded with a good meal.

BARBFISH

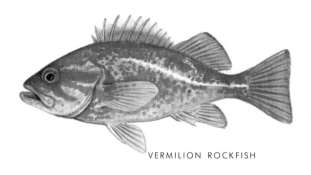

VERMILION ROCKFISH

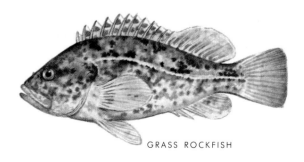

GRASS ROCKFISH

SCORPIONFISHES, *continued*

BOCACCIO   To 3 ft.
An important predator of fish along the Pacific Coast, the Bocaccio is preyed upon, in turn, by sharks, sea lions, and toothed whales. It is less heavy-bodied than most scorpionfishes, and the corner of its *large mouth* is *farther back* than the eye. Young Bocaccio (not shown), which have brown spots, are often caught in shallow water. The adults live in deeper water and are caught less often. The wide-ranging Bocaccio is found from Kodiak Island, Alaska, to Baja California. Anglers should be wary of the mildly venomous spines on the dorsal and anal fins.

YELLOWTAIL ROCKFISH   To 2 ft., 2 in.
This is one of the few open-water scorpionfishes. It ranges over deep reefs in schools from Kodiak Island, Alaska, to San Diego. The Yellowtail is distinguished by its slim shape and its *somewhat yellow fins.* On its sides, above the lateral line, are several *pale rectangular patches.* This is a feature it shares with other members of its family, such as the Olive Rockfish (not shown). The dorsal and anal fins contain a mild venom.

GOLDEN REDFISH   To 1 ft., 8 in.
Together with the closely related Deepwater Redfish, the Golden Redfish is marketed in fresh fish shops as "Ocean Perch." As with the Red Snapper (see p. 80), its red color hints at its deep ocean habitat. In the blue depths, a red fish appears black, enabling it to hide from its prey. The Golden Redfish is found in cold waters from Greenland to New Jersey. It is also found near Scandinavia and the British Isles. On both sides of the Atlantic it is an important commercial fish. Like all scorpionfishes, the Redfish grows very slowly, making it vulnerable to over-fishing.

BOCACCIO

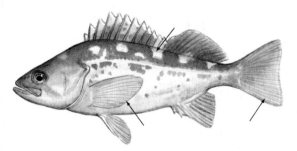

YELLOWTAIL ROCKFISH

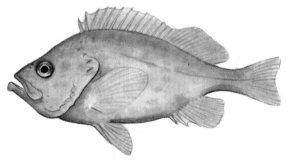

GOLDEN REDFISH
(OCEAN PERCH)

SEAROBINS

NORTHERN SEAROBIN To 1 ft., 4 in.

Like their relatives, the scorpionfishes, searobins are mostly bottom-dwellers. The Northern Searobin has distinctive *winglike pectoral fins* with *3 fingerlike free rays* at the front. These are used to feel in the mud for worms and other small prey. This fish can also be identified by the *black spot* on the 1st dorsal fin. The Northern Searobin lives from Nova Scotia to central Florida.

SCULPINS

Sculpins have the typical look of bottom-dwellers: a long, low profile; large pectoral fins; and eyes set high on the head. When a sculpin spreads its pectoral fins, water flows over its body, pressing it to the bottom. Sculpins lack gas-filled swim bladders, a feature that also helps keep them on the bottom. They live in both fresh and salt water.

CABEZON To 3 ft., 3 in.

One of the world's largest sculpins, the Cabezon is caught throughout its range, from southern Alaska to Baja California. The Cabezon is good to eat but its eggs are poisonous. This mottled sculpin has *fleshy growths* above each eye.

SEA RAVEN To 2 ft.

This sculpin has a *ragged, high dorsal fin* with *many fleshy tabs*. There are also *fleshy projections* on the chin and head. The Sea Raven lives from Labrador to Chesapeake Bay, in water ranging from 6 ft. to 600 ft. deep. It is also noted for its prickly skin.

BANDED SCULPIN To 5 in.

One of the many North American freshwater sculpins, the Banded Sculpin inhabits clear rivers and streams, from the southern Midwest to Alabama. It sports *several bars* on its back and sides, and *rows of dark spots* on its 2nd dorsal, anal, and tail fins. The 1st dorsal fin has *dark blotches*. This sculpin's *wide, fanlike pectoral fins* are unusual for a freshwater fish in its range.

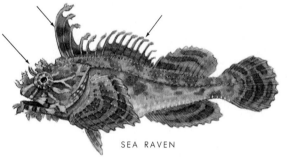

NORTHERN SEAROBIN

CABEZON

SEA RAVEN

BANDED SCULPIN

POACHERS

STURGEON POACHER To 1 ft.
Although it has a similar-looking head, this little poacher is not related to the sturgeons (see p. 20). Like most poachers, it is found in the North Pacific, from southern Alaska to northern California. Its *mouth is under its snout,* and is surrounded by *whiskerlike cirri.*

GREENLINGS
Greenlings are found only in the North Pacific. They are related to scorpionfishes (see p. 106) but lack the venomous spines. Many greenlings are quite variable in color.

PAINTED GREENLING To 10 in.
This greenling comes in 2 color phases: light grayish brown and quite dark. Both phases have *broad, dark bars* that extend out *onto the fins.* This fish occasionally bears *many small white spots.* It ranges from Kodiak Island, Alaska, to Baja California. Although it is sometimes confused with the unrelated Treefish (not shown), the Painted Greenling has *fleshy cirri* above the eyes.

KELP GREENLING To 1 ft., 9 in.
Found from the Aleutian Islands to southern California, this greenling is sought by anglers throughout its range, but is common only in the northern part, where it has some importance as a food fish. The sexes are differently patterned — the female is *gray-brown* with *small gold or brown spots,* and the male is *covered with light blue spots.* Both have "*eyebrows*" *of fleshy cirri.* The female attaches her egg mass to rocks. The male guards the eggs until they hatch.

LINGCOD To 5 ft.
This large greenling (which is not a cod) ranges from Kodiak Island to Baja California. The Lingcod is an important sport and food fish in the North Pacific. It is *long and slender,* with a *projecting lower jaw.* On close inspection, the Lingcod's *spots* resemble those in a jaguar's coat.

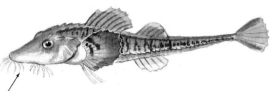

STURGEON POACHER

color
varies

PAINTED GREENLING

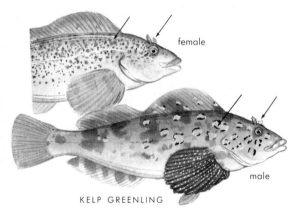

female

male

KELP GREENLING

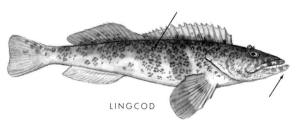

LINGCOD

LUMPFISHES AND SNAILFISHES

LUMPFISH To 2 ft.

Loosely translated, the scientific name of the Lumpfish *(Cyclopterus lumpus)* means "the lumpy thing with round fins." "Lumpy" is certainly the first thought that springs to mind upon seeing a Lumpfish. The body is vaguely *football-shaped* and *covered with bumps*, and the pelvic fins are fused into a *round suction disk* (the "round fins" of the scientific name). This disk, which is a characteristic of the entire lumpfish family, is used to attach the fish to rocks. It also accounts for the alternate name of the fishes in this group: Lumpsucker. The Lumpfish is found on both sides of the North Atlantic, from Hudson Bay to New Jersey on the North American side. Its flesh is not often eaten, but its eggs are quite valuable as caviar.

TIDEPOOL SNAILFISH To 7 in.

Some scientists place the snailfishes in the lumpfish family, and some group them in a family of their own. Like the lumpfishes, the snailfishes have a *suction disk* formed from the pelvic fins. The Tidepool Snailfish uses this disk to cling to rocks in the tidepools where it lives. This prevents it from being dashed against the rocks by waves. Found from Kodiak Island to northern California, the Tidepool Snailfish is a slender little fish with *nearly mirror-image dorsal and anal fins.* At the *front* of the dorsal fin is a *small peak.*

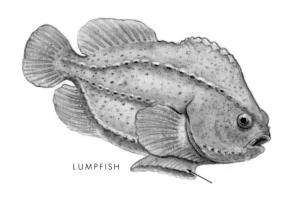

LUMPFISH

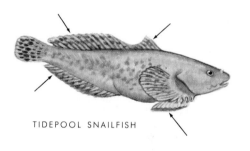

TIDEPOOL SNAILFISH

Flatfishes

This group includes the flounders, halibuts, and soles. The sides of all flatfishes are very flattened. These fishes always lie on the same side (either left or right, depending on the species), with both eyes on the upper side. The young hatch as "normal" fishes. As they grow, one eye migrates to the other side, the body flattens, and the swim bladder disappears. No fishes are better adapted to bottom life. Most flatfishes are prized for food.

GULF FLOUNDER   To 15 in.

With the *3 dark eyespots* on its upper (left) side, the Gulf Flounder is easily recognized. It lives on muddy bottoms near the coast, from North Carolina to Texas. This important food and game fish would be even more valuable except for its small size.

PEACOCK FLOUNDER   To 1½ ft.

This flounder is found near coral reefs and mangroves, in warm water from Florida to Brazil. Its upper (left) side is covered with beautiful *blue rings.* Matching blue spots appear on the head and fins. Occasionally, there are 2–3 dark smudges along the lateral line.

CALIFORNIA HALIBUT   To 5 ft.

This large Pacific fish is very popular for both sport and food. The California Halibut is found on soft bottoms, from Washington to Baja California. The eyes are usually on the left side, but are occasionally found on the right. The mouth is *large* — the corner reaches farther back than the eye.

STARRY FLOUNDER   To 3 ft.

The eyes of this flounder can be on either the right or the left side (both shown). Its striking markings include *dark bars* on its dorsal, anal, and tail fins, and star-shaped, modified scales on its upper side. The upper side is dark, sometimes nearly black. This popular sport fish is found near shore, from the Arctic to Santa Barbara, California, and across the Pacific near Japan.

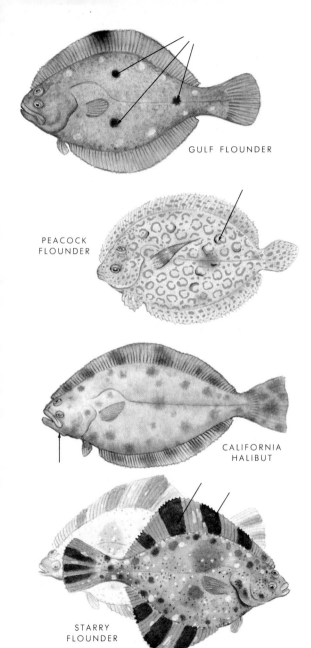

GULF FLOUNDER

PEACOCK FLOUNDER

CALIFORNIA HALIBUT

STARRY FLOUNDER

FLATFISHES, *continued*

PACIFIC HALIBUT
To 8¾ ft.

This is the largest West Coast flatfish. The eyes are usually on the right side. The Pacific Halibut has a *slightly forked tail* and a darkly mottled upper side. This valuable commercial and sport fish is found on soft bottoms, from the Bering Sea to southern California.

ROCK SOLE
To 2 ft.

The Rock Sole lives on rocky or soft bottoms, from the Bering Sea to southern California. It can be identified by its *lateral line*, which is arched over its pectoral fin and has a short dorsal branch. A good food fish, the Rock Sole is especially important in Canada.

WINTER FLOUNDER
To 2 ft.

This flounder lives on muddy or sandy bottoms, from Labrador to Georgia. It is called the Winter Flounder because it often retreats to cold, deep water in the summer and reappears in shallower water close to shore in the winter. An important food fish, the Winter Flounder has an *unusually small mouth* for a flatfish. Its body color varies from dark green to dark red to black, with or without mottling.

HOGCHOKER
To 8 in.

This little sole, too small to be commercially important, is a delicious delicacy for the angler. It lives in shallow, nearshore water, from Maine to Mexico. The Hogchoker is oval, with a blunt head and 7–8 *narrow, dark bars*. Its eyes are on the right side. The name "Hogchoker" dates from colonial times. It is said to come from the rough scales, which could choke hogs fed on discarded fish on the beach.

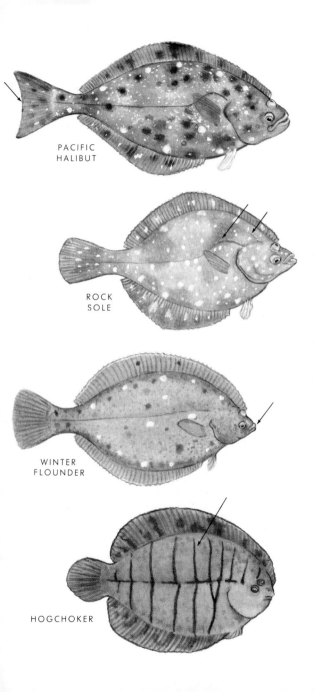

PACIFIC
HALIBUT

ROCK
SOLE

WINTER
FLOUNDER

HOGCHOKER

Leatherjackets and Relatives

The leatherjacket family is made up of the filefishes and the triggerfishes. Unlike most other fishes, members of this family swim by moving their anal fin and 2nd dorsal fin. The tail fin is used for steering. A leatherjacket's skin is covered with microscopic scales, giving it a velvety feel.

SCRAWLED FILEFISH   To 3 ft.

This fish will sometimes position itself with its head down, which helps conceal it in seagrass. It is a long fish with a very long snout and a "scrawled" pattern of *blue lines and spots* mixed with *black spots*. Found in seagrass beds, the Scrawled Filefish ranges from New England to Brazil.

QUEEN TRIGGERFISH   To 2 ft.

The beautiful Queen Triggerfish ranges from Massachusetts to Brazil, but is only common in warm water. It lives near rocky and coral reefs and artificial "reefs," such as pilings and jetties. Although it feeds on a wide variety of invertebrates, the Queen prefers the long-spined sea urchins. It flips an urchin over, attacking the unprotected underside. *Two blue lines*, one starting at the snout and the other at the blue-ringed mouth, are characteristic of the Queen Triggerfish. Like all triggerfishes, it has 3 stout dorsal spines that can be locked into place as a defense against predators.

BLACK DURGON   To 20 in.

The Black Durgon is black with a *pale blue line* along the base of the anal fin and the 2nd dorsal fin. Sometimes a cast of dark green or bronze can be seen in its scales. This triggerfish is found on both coasts. In the Atlantic, it ranges from the Gulf of Mexico to Florida; in the Pacific, it ranges from San Diego to Colombia. Usually it lives on the outer edges of reefs, where it feeds on algae and floating plants, occasionally adding animal food to its diet.

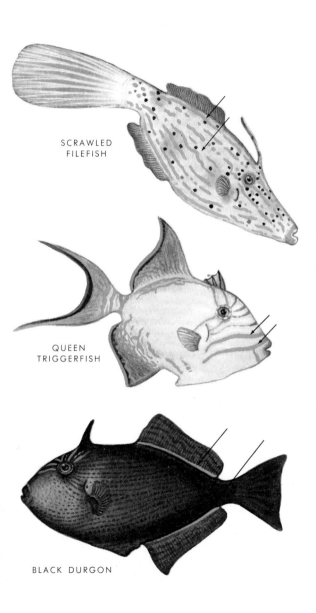

SCRAWLED
FILEFISH

QUEEN
TRIGGERFISH

BLACK DURGON

BOXFISHES

Members of the boxfish family are encased in a hard, shell-like sheath made from bony, modified scales. They are slow swimmers, but are effectively protected from predators by their armor.

SCRAWLED COWFISH   To 1½ ft.

With a pair of sharp *horns over each eye* and another pair projecting from the lower rear corners of its body, the Scrawled Cowfish would be a thorny mouthful for any predator. Its yellowish body is covered by a *blue scrawl pattern*. Found in shallow, grassy water from Massachusetts to Brazil, this fish feeds on soft-bodied invertebrates.

TRUNKFISH   To 1¾ ft.

The Trunkfish *lacks the horned head* of the Cowfish. On its rear, however, is a sharp pair of thorny projections. The color pattern of this fish is variable, ranging from brownish olive with dark blotches and pale spots to a deep, marbled bluish gray in older adults. The Trunkfish inhabits seagrass beds and coral reefs, from Massachusetts to Brazil.

PUFFERS AND SPINY PUFFERS

Rather than relying on rigid armor for protection as their boxfish relatives do, the puffers and spiny puffers suddenly inflate their bodies with water or air when they need to defend themselves. The spiny puffers' spines provide further protection from predators.

OCEANIC PUFFER   To 2 ft.

Unlike most other puffers, the Oceanic lives in the open ocean. Found from Newfoundland to Bermuda and from northern California south, this fish is also quite common throughout the world's open seas. Like many other open-ocean fishes, this fish has a strongly contrasting dark back and white belly. This helps to hide it from predators whether it is seen from above or below. Its *lower tail-fin lobe is longer* than the upper lobe.

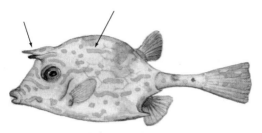

SCRAWLED COWFISH

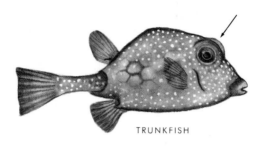

TRUNKFISH

OCEAN PUFFER

NORTHERN PUFFER   To 1 ft.

Sold in seafood shops as "sea squab," the
Northern is one of the few puffers that is
non-toxic and safe to eat. Anglers should
take no chances, however, as the Northern
can be confused with the toxic Bandtail Puffer (not shown). The Northern has many
small spots and several *dark bars and
blotches*. It inhabits protected coastal
waters, such as bays and estuaries, from
Newfoundland to northern Florida.

PORCUPINEFISH   To 3 ft.

The Porcupinefish is found throughout the
world in the warm waters of the Atlantic,
Indian, and Pacific oceans. In the New
World it ranges from Massachusetts to Brazil in the Atlantic, and from San Diego to
Chile in the Pacific. The Porcupinefish is
easily recognized by its *long, spiky spines*,
which become erect when the fish puffs
itself up. Only the smaller Balloonfish (not
shown), which has longer spines on the
head, is very similar. The Porcupinefish
crushes snails, sea urchins, and crabs with
its strong beak.

STRIPED BURRFISH   To 10 in.

The *short spines* of the Striped Burrfish
stay erect even when it is not inflated. This
fish gets its name from its *dark brown
stripes* as well as from its burrlike spiny
covering. Ranging from North Carolina to
Brazil, the Striped Burrfish is very common
in seagrass beds during the summer. In the
winter, it retreats to deeper water. Young
specimens are popular aquarium fishes.

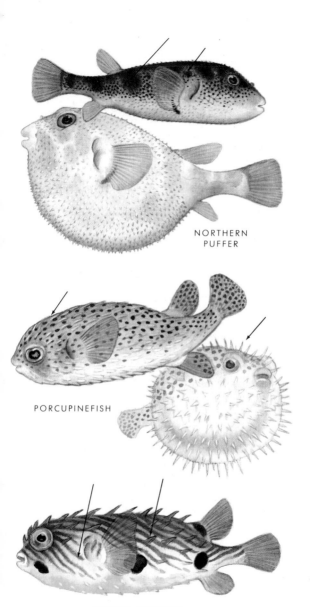

NORTHERN
PUFFER

PORCUPINEFISH

STRIPED BURRFISH

OCEAN SUNFISH

To 10 ft.

The gigantic Ocean Sunfish is a peculiar-looking fish. At first glance, it appears to be all head. The very compressed body comes to an abrupt stop behind the head, and is fringed by a scalloped tail fin. This fish swims by sculling with its high dorsal and anal fins. It lacks scales and, although it is classified as a bony fish, it has a skeleton made up largely of cartilage. The Ocean Sunfish lives in the open ocean from Newfoundland to South America and feeds on jellyfish. Its young have globular bodies covered with spines and look nothing like the adults.

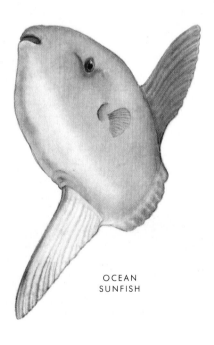

OCEAN
SUNFISH

INDEX